The Lure of the City

GW00360687

The Lure of the City

From Slums to Suburbs

Edited by
Austin Williams and Alastair Donald

PlutoPress
www.plutobooks.com

First published 2011 by Pluto Press
345 Archway Road, London N6 5AA

www.plutobooks.com

Distributed in the United States of America exclusively by
Palgrave Macmillan, a division of St. Martin's Press LLC,
175 Fifth Avenue, New York, NY 10010

British Library Cataloguing in Publication Data
A catalogue record for this book is available from the British Library

ISBN   978 0 7453 3178 2   Hardback
ISBN   978 0 7453 3177 5   Paperback

Library of Congress Cataloging in Publication Data applied for

This book is printed on paper suitable for recycling and made from fully managed
and sustained forest sources. Logging, pulping and manufacturing processes are
expected to conform to the environmental standards of the country of origin.

10   9   8   7   6   5   4   3   2   1

Designed and produced for Pluto Press by Chase Publishing Services Ltd
Typeset from disk by Stanford DTP Services, Northampton, England
Simultaneously printed digitally by CPI Antony Rowe, Chippenham, UK and
Edwards Bros in the United States of America

Contents

Introduction
The Paradoxical City

Alastair Donald

… we had everything before us, we had nothing before us, we were all going direct to Heaven, we were all going direct the other way.

Charles Dickens, *A Tale of Two Cities*

Cities, according to the United Nations, are 'dynamic centres of creativity, commerce and culture'.[1] Are they not sometimes hectic, tense, polluted and crowded? But then again, are these two characterisations mutually exclusive? Aren't they *both* what cities are meant to be?

For the first time in human history, 3 billion people – more than half of the world's population – live in cities. The number of urban dwellers is predicted to reach 5 billion by 2030, at which time the urban populations in the developing world will be four times as large as those in the more economically developed countries. Yet while this explosion of urban life could be greeted enthusiastically as a sign of progress and development – moving people off the land and out of back-breaking labour – rapid urbanisation is in fact often seen through the contemporary prism of social, political and ecological concerns: overpopulation, fears over the breakdown of traditional communities, and the dangers cities create for the broader environment, to name but a few. Within the West, as cities grow, it seems that with them grows a heightened sense of social unrest, violence, urban blight and a community breakdown. So much for architect Daniel Libeskind's belief that 'cities are the greatest creations of humanity'.[2]

This book explores the paradoxes and contradictions, opportunities and challenges of an urban world. Is the city the place of anonymity, or of civic engagement? Will developing countries lose cultural identity in their transition to urban economies? If so, will it be worth it? Are cities dynamic centres

1

of innovation, or outdated modes of organisation? Are cities sociable, or anti-social? Should historic centres be conserved, or demolished to create new ones? Are cities too impersonal, or are they welcoming? Is a stress-free, uncongested city a contradiction in terms? Is that even what we should be striving for? Do cities encourage liberal free expression, or are they places of conformity? Why, in this, the 'Urban Age',[3] aren't we building new cities in the West? Conversely, are emerging economies developing their urban centres too fast, with scant regard for the long term? And what about those cities in decline – should they be saved, or buried?

THE CHALLENGES

If 'cities are at the centre of human civilization and invention',[4] then they certainly cannot be stripped of the very forces that make them so: the complexities, contradictions and conflicts that shape all human affairs, and which on a daily basis shape the lives of the billions of men and women who now form *Homo sapiens urbanus*.[5] Since classical times, the city has been a refuge both for the innovator and the disbeliever;[6] an escape from a feudal world, but also the place where dreams could be pursued, where change, contingency and incompleteness were persistent features.[7] It is the contestation at the heart of urban life that is of interest to our writers. Central to this book, therefore, is the paradox of unity: 'Modernity can be said to unite all mankind. But it is a paradoxical unity, a unity of disunity: it pours us all into a maelstrom of perpetual disintegration and renewal, of struggle and contradiction, of ambiguity and anguish.'[8]

At a time when the population of the world's cities is swollen every single week by more than a million migrants – mostly in the cities of the developing world – a number of the chapters in this book consider the latest challenges of the urban emergence and the transition to a modern world.

For some years, change has often been at its most rapid and exhilarating in cities shaped by the dynamic economies of China and India. Migrants often take their place on the sprawled edges or in the dense centres of cities, and whatever the potential problems, the sense of exhilaration that results from leaving a rural area in order to tap into the world's urban networks is unmistakable. For those swapping a village for a tower block, and work in the fields for a job as a cleaner, a typically resolute response is: 'Life is much better – we are urbanised and have become proper citizens.'[9]

Yet in Chapter 1, 'The Dynamic City', Alan Hudson, Director of Oxford University's Leadership Programme for China, reports that the relationship between urbanisation and citizenship is considerably more complex than that. In economically dynamic Chinese cities, many are only 'citizens' in a formal sense, and millions of migrants with no formal registration are not citizens at all. Certainly, the onset of the modern world has destroyed traditional relationships and hierarchies, but does city air make the new urban masses free? Hudson's essay explores the tensions and opportunities that exist in cities operating at new scales of interconnection, where global meets the local, but the state rarely meets the citizen.

The emerging urban centres of Africa are less well celebrated, but their growth is such that the continent has become the fastest-urbanising region in the world. Around 2030, it will cease to be predominantly rural.[10] The focus for discussion in Africa (and of many other cities of the South and East) has become the slums. Regionally, Sub-Saharan Africa has the largest slum population, in both absolute and proportional terms, accommodating 200 million people (62 per cent of its urban population).[11] If the setting for urban life is where garbage mountains meet open sewers, then why do migrants continue to make their way there?

In Chapter 2, 'The Emerging City', I explore what author Edward Glaeser terms an 'urban poverty paradox' – the flow of poor people into already poor areas.[12] In the nineteenth century, when migrants landed in Lower East Manhattan and the rookery of St Giles in London, it was recognised that, while they were dirty and crowded places, they were also rich in opportunity. So does the enormous size and continued growth of slums today set them apart from the past? Is it – or should it be – necessary for today's urban migrants to go through the same experiences as their migrant forefathers?

It is the tensions, conflicts and contradictions so central to the dynamic of cities that we grapple with throughout this book. In doing so, we avoid succumbing to the numbers game that paints pictures with statistics. The architect Rem Koolhaas bemoaned the fact that urbanists no longer develop theories of what to do with cities, but merely write portraits in the hope of understanding them.[13] While data are important, the welter of information published on densities, pollution, travel distances, carbon emissions, crime, and so on, is indicative of the tendency of today's urbanists to fall back on 'data' as a means to justify, and sometimes post-rationalise, their position. In this sense, statistics have become a crutch, a substitute for critical enquiry and engagement with urban issues. All too often, people in cities – and their social relations – are reduced to numbers. This book discusses data, but we hope that we deal with uncomfortable political and professional realities, too.

One reason for challenging conventional wisdom is to get beyond the sham objective standards at the heart of much research, and uncover important aspects of the debate that often remain unexplored. For example, in Chapter 3, 'The Crowded City', Patrick Hayes points out that apparently neutral categories of investigation related to overcrowding are less the product of science-based neutrality than of subjective prejudice. As Hayes reveals, the issue is less about the number of people we pack onto trains, roads, and so on, but rather about how we view public space, our fellow citizens, and indeed our common humanity. Why today is the crowded metropolis something to fear rather than to accept, or even celebrate?

MAKE NO BIG PLANS?

As Michael Owens points out in Chapter 4, 'The Planned City', during the age of the urban revolution, planners often operated in the belief that not only could the urban environment be *adapted* to meet the needs of a growing population, but that cities, and the prospects of citizens, could be *transformed* through bold visions for comprehensive change. Today, in western cities at least, Daniel Burnham's famous maxim, 'Make No Little Plans', seems no longer to apply, and planning has also ceased to exist as a matter of grand ambition, instead celebrating cities as organically evolving settlements, and prioritising engaging communities in local consultation exercises.

Given that many bold visions of the past were developed and perpetrated by powerful, unelected figures – Burnham's 1909 Plan of Chicago, for example, was produced in collaboration with the Commercial Club of Chicago – is there something to celebrate about the emergence in the 1960s of community planning, which brought communities into the discussion on the future of cities? On the other hand, although the bold visions of Haussmann-esque figures may not have been expressed in democratic terms, the paradoxical result was social improvement and human progress. Does today's privileging of incremental change over large-scale intervention and 'thinking big' represent a democratic turn, or signal a broader collapse in confidence that humanity can shape the world according to its desires?

One conundrum raised by those who favour a 'hands-off' approach to planning is how the phenomenon of urban decline – or what has been called 'shrinking cities' – should be addressed.[14] Even as the world grows steadily more urbanised, in the West a discussion has broken out over 'declinism'.[15] At the heart of this discussion lies the American city of Detroit, whose population has plunged by 25 per cent in the last decade.[16] Where once a response to decline might have been ambitious plans for regeneration, nowadays many commentators seem content to ruminate over the 'destiny of cities'.[17]

Clearly, urban decline is nothing new, Rome being only the most obvious early example. But recently, not only have contemporary attitudes to decline become more fatalistic; a new cultural appetite for the imagery of urban decay suggests that something else is being played out. From Greek tragedies to the Grand Tour, myths of urban ruin have loomed large in the cultural imagination for a long time. So is it true, as one commentator alleges, that ruins are 'good metaphors for human nature, for our ability to create and destroy'?[18] Has Detroit suffered a man-made Hurricane Katrina?[19] Does it offer a sober lesson as to what the future holds?

As Steve Nash and Austin Williams point out in Chapter 5, 'The Historic City', ruins and symbols of the past are often integrated into new cityscapes, and have become part of the system of cultural representations of cities. According to one reviewer of *Robinson In Ruins*, the latest in a series of films by Patrick Keiller, although ruins are mainly associated with nostalgia, Keiller portrays them through vital and optimistic eyes.[20]

Nash and Williams argue for the importance of differentiating between nostalgia, which may or may not have been part of traditional approaches to historic preservation, and the selective use of fragments of the urban past which are peddled by the 'urban memory' industry today. 'Conserving cityscapes', if it is necessary at all, should be conducted according to a considered debate that leads society to decide what it values, and how much of the past is worth bringing into the future. The 'urban memory' industry, by contrast, appears to offer a compelling illustration of the inability of society to envisage the future. Instead of an ambitious search for universal truths, it endorses many values that reflect the absence of a future. It is a fragmentary, therapeutic and self-indulgent prostitution of the past.

REASSERTING URBAN AUTONOMY

Recent changes in legislation governing the function of urban spaces are examined in Chapter 6, 'The Sanitized City', as part of a broader historic set of cultural changes. Tony Pierce and Austin Williams explore in detail the reasons – in different eras – for codes and legislation that act to the detriment of individual autonomy. They reveal that interventions which at first might appear comparable are really motivated by very different objectives.

Take, for example, the codes of conduct and rules that govern movement. In London agreement as to how to use pavements was established in Victorian times.[21] Since then we have become used to injunctions to stand on the right-hand side of moving escalators, and control over the volume and flow of traffic has been imposed by the introduction of parking meters and traffic lights. All of these rules and devices to control movement within the city are generally accepted. On the other hand, the Congestion Charge, another measure to control movement, has generated considerable animosity. In London, the Western extension was overturned, while the proposed introduction of charging in Manchester and Edinburgh was rejected by substantial majorities. An examination of new urban rules reveals much about the changing understanding of individual freedoms, as well as a shift in contemporary views on what represents the 'public good', where individual autonomy is assumed to be at odds with the civic and environmental values asserted by the state.

The paradox that we point to in the contemporary city is that of public space without public life. Chapter 6 highlights one of the most important areas for investigation in the book: the question of the relationship between the citizen and the state, and between the public and private domains. Much criticism in recent years has been focused on the privatisation of public space, which is now overregulated and under surveillance. However, the authors identify an important shift, and reveal that, while it is fair to criticise the privatisation of public space, we ignore at our peril the fact that the private domain of the individual is now becoming public property.

In China, for example, the United Nations points out that 'centres of rapid industrial growth and wealth creation [are] often accompanied by harmful waste and pollution'.[22] It is alleged that dirty air and water cause the premature deaths of 760,000 Chinese each year.[23] So what should be made of the Chinese motorists who ignore 'No Car Day' and proceed to go about their business?[24] Do they stand condemned for a lack of concern for the environment and their own health? Or is the promise of a better material quality of life more important than the sins of emission? Is it a good thing that some citizens assert their autonomy and refuse to bow to such injunctions with the dutiful compliance often exhibited in the west? Or is it simply irresponsible behaviour that deserves to be punished?

IMAGINING THE FUTURE

According to Richard Rogers, one of the world's premier architects, 'the dangers of over-development are as serious as the dangers of under-development'.[25] As a starting point for imaging the future city, Rogers's statement of the need for constraints is revealing, given that architects have traditionally operated on the assumption (now widely viewed as arrogance) that design could help overcome supposedly objective limits to growth and development. Yet, as Austin Williams points out in Chapter 7, 'The Eco-City', the city of the future is now invariably prefixed with 'eco' to signify acceptance of environmental limits and the need for caution, precaution, fewer choices and more regulation – often meaning, ironically, that developing cities are intentionally underdeveloped.

Recognising a culture of conservatism in architecture, Williams makes a strong case for rediscovering a commitment to open-mindedness, inquisitiveness and critical awareness. Regardless of how one views what they built, as the author Deyan Sudjic has written, architects today are devoid of the confidence exhibited by the pioneer Modernists, 'a generation that was freed from the luxury of self-doubt'.[26] As Williams and Karl Sharro point out in Chapter 8, 'The Visionary City', a vibrant, future-orientated imagination once revelled in the forward momentum of society – brimming with a sense of impatience, a reflection of a desire to escape the constraints of both past and present. In the course of the twentieth century, plans were developed for walking cities, mobile cities, floating cities, submersible cities, flying cities and space cities. The 'walking city' was a city that walked, literally conveying its population to new locations at their whim, simply for a change of scenery. Today, the 'walking city' has come to mean simply a city in which you walk! Architecture today seems to be characterised by an absence of vision and a reluctance to challenge the established framework of constraint.

MAKING HUMANITY VISIBLE

Asking whether cities are a burden or a blessing, the United Nations has indicated that '[t]he battle for a sustainable environmental future is being waged primarily in the world's cities. Right now, cities draw together many of Earth's major environmental problems: population growth, pollution, resource degradation and waste generation.'[27]

Unfortunately, in this pessimistic view of the future city, people are reduced to little more than a problem to be managed. Where once cities were associated with advances in human civilisation, today the quest for a 'sustainable environmental future' revolves around a diminished view of mankind, a view of humanity as merely the consumers of resources and emitters of waste. Such a misanthropic, limited and austere vision is entirely hostile to the goals of human progress, autonomy, social and technological experimentation, and wealth-creation, which cities should aim to embody.

If cities are mankind's greatest creation, then perhaps the greatest paradox of the city today is the very attempt to impoverish all that is human. As an alternative, this book attempts to make humanity visible. We stake out the case for cities as agglomerations of human dreams.

NOTES

1. United Nations Cyberschoolbus, *Backgrounder 5: Governance, Participation and Partnerships*, Global Teaching and Learning Project, at <www.un.org/cyberschoolbus/habitat/background/bg5.asp>.

2. Daniel Libeskind, quoted on CNN, 'The Rise and Rise of the Skyscraper', 4 July 2005.

3. The Urban Age, at <www.urban-age.net>.

4. Anne Power, 'The Changing Face of Cities', in United Nations Environment Programme and World Conservation Monitoring Centre, *Environment on the Edge*, UNEP, 2006, p. 49, at <www.

unep-wcmc-apps.org/resources/PDFs/EOTEII/EnvtonEdge05-06HR.pdf>.

5. UN-HABITAT, 'State of the World's Cities 2010/2011 – Cities for All: Bridging the Urban Divide', Earthscan, 2010, p. x.

6. James E. Vance Jr, *The Scene of Man*, Harper's College Press, 1977, p. 12.

7. Thomas Bender, *The Unfinished City: New York and The Metropolitan Idea*, New York: New Press, 2002, p. xiv.

8. Marshal Berman, *All That Is Solid Melts Into Air*, New York: Verso, p. 15.

9. Mick Brown, 'America and China: The Eagle & The Dragon Part Three', *Daily Telegraph*, 12 July 2009.

10. UN-HABITAT, 'State of the World's African Cities 2010: Governance, Inequality and Urban Land Markets', UN-HABITAT/UNEP, November 2010.

11. UN-HABITAT, '"Urban Trends: 227 Million Escape Slums" – State of the World's Cities 2010/2011: Bridging the Urban Divide', UN-HABITAT, 18 March 2010.

12. Edward Glaeser, *The Triumph of the City: How Our Greatest Invention Makes Us Richer, Smarter, Greener, Healthier And Happier*, New York: Macmillan, 2011, p. 76.

13. Rem Koolhaas, 'Dilemmas in the Evolution of the City', speech delivered in London to Commisson for Architecture and the Built Environment (CABE), London, 16 January 2006.

14. 'Shrinking Cities', at <www.shrinkingcities.com/index.php?L=1>.

15. Gwen Webber, 'This is the Motor City', *Blueprint*, 22 March 2011.

16. Katharine Q. Seeleye, 'Detroit Census Confirms a Desertion Like No Other', *New York Times*, 22 March 2011, at <www.nytimes.com/2011/03/23/us/23detroit.html?_r=2>.

17. Victor Davis Hanson, 'The Destiny of Cities', *City Journal* 20: 4 (Autumn 2010).

18. Prospero, *The Ruins of Detroit: Up from the Ashes*, Economist Online, 3 March 2011.

19. John Patrick Leary, 'Detriotism', *Guernica*, January 2011.

20. Natre Wannathepsakul, 'Film Review: Robinson in Ruins', *Blueprint*, 21 March 2011.

21. Jerry White, *London in the Nineteenth Century*, Vintage, p. 121.

22. Ban Ki-moon, 'Foreword', in UN-HABITAT, 'State of the World's Cities 2010/2011 – Cities for All: Bridging the Urban Divide', Earthscan, 2010, p. x.

23. BBC News, 'China "Buried Smog Death Finding"', 3 July 2007.

24. BBC News, 'Beijing Drivers Ignore No Car Day', 22 September 2007.

25. Richard Rogers and Ann Powers, *Cities for a Small Country*, Faber & Faber, 2000, p. 139.

26. Deyan Sudjic, 'Cities on the Edge of Chaos', *Observer*, 9 March 2008.

27. United Nations Population Fund, 'State of the World's Population 2007: Urbanization and Sustainability in the 21st Century', at <www.unfpa.org/swp/2007/english/chapter_5/index.html>.

1
The Dynamic City
Citizens Make Cities

Alan Hudson

All human progress, political, moral, or intellectual, is inseparable from
material progression.

Auguste Comte, 'The Positive Philosophy of Auguste Comte'

The central concern in this chapter is to re-pose the question
of how a city might come to be, or to be defined as, dynamic.
'Re-pose' because, although at one level it may seem to be a
semantic quibble, the physical fabric of cities ultimately amounts
only to a large collection of inanimate objects: citizens make
cities, not the other way round.

It may seem strange, therefore, to illustrate my argument
through the example of Chinese cities in general, and of Shanghai
in particular. On the one hand, the inhabitants of Chinese cities
are 'citizens' in only a formal sense – indeed, millions of migrant
workers are not citizens at all. Under the household registration
(*hukou*) system in China, every person has a permanent place
of registered residence that can only be changed with official
approval. The terms 'migrant' and 'floating' population denote
those people who leave their places of residence without officially
moving their *hukou*. Historically, this has been difficult to do,
leaving the migrant without much entitlement to social provision
– although in recent years this has changed, at least at the
legislative level.

On the other hand, the Chinese city – through aggressive
planning, state-sponsored market intervention and economic
growth – is to all intents and purposes, and certainly in relation
to the contemporary developed world, singularly dynamic. The
peculiar feature of contemporary China is the close association
of a central Five Year Plan (FYP), written in detail for national,

provincial and municipal levels of government, with a capitalist market ring-fenced by state authority. The quintessential relationship is between a party official and a property developer, although they may be the same person.

Thus, the argument is not that planning, growth and action on a grand scale are not important – far from it. The reconfiguration of my argument is rather that the relationship between, on the one hand, technical expertise and the activity of experts, and, on the other, the active understanding, involvement and participatory collaboration of citizens, both as individuals and as groups, is out of joint. There is, in a sense, a double dynamic. But it works in parallel rather than in series, and therefore undermines the mutual reinforcement of the life of the city (the citizen) with its activity (planning). There is no clear mechanism for effective communication between the city plan and the activities of the population. At the same time, the inhabitants' activities are predominantly in the economic and not the social or political spheres. Such activities have a huge economic impact, but in a sense they happen behind the back of the plan. Similarly, large developmental projects, although planned, happen with little regard to the overall social environment of the city.

Chinese officials are not oblivious to this contradiction – in relation to both the actual erosion of trust and legitimacy in their system, and the potential for civil dissatisfaction and opposition. The need to reconcile economic development with social justice is central to both the 11th and 12th Five-Year Plans (those for 2006–10 and 2011–15). But it is perceived as being a technical problem with a technical solution; there is little or no perception that the separation of economic growth from public engagement may not only be problematic, but that it actually detracts from the vitality and ambience of the city.

HONGQIAO CENTRAL BUSINESS DISTRICT

In December 2010, I hosted a delegation from Shanghai and chaired a seminar on urbanisation. The purpose of the delegation's visit was to glean ideas, and policies, for the development of a

new business district in Shanghai, Shanghai Hongqiao Central
Business District (CBD).

The delegation leader – who had been seconded from the
Chinese Executive Leadership Academy, Pudong, a national party
school for the training of city mayors, young leaders and state
enterprise executives – was in charge of research and planning
for the Hongqiao project. He explained he would coordinate the
activities of 23 government and parastatal agencies, including
eight police forces. Nevertheless, the research phase would be
concluded in 18 months, the plan presented by 2012, and the
project completed in the following five years.

After watching the promotional video for Hongqiao and
listening to the delegation leader's polite request for advice, the
assembled experts and academics offered their comments: 'Don't
have any roads'; 'Buy my software for the central monitoring
of energy use in public buildings'; 'Think about solving the
technical problems of the future and not just of today'. The
delegation listened politely. My impression was that buried
within the comments might be some useful advice that could be
incorporated into the master plan. But my overwhelming sense
was that there was nothing new or exciting on offer.

Hongqiao is already developed as a transport hub. It is the site
of Shanghai's second, more domestically orientated airport, and
will be the terminus for the high-speed rail link to Beijing (4.5
hours), Hangzhou (38 minutes) and Nanjing (42 minutes). This
multidirectional, high-speed network will complete the fusion
of the Yangtze River Delta's 'half-hour circle'. The daily traffic
flow is projected at 1.4 million people.

The current population of the core area of 3.7 square kilometres
is 50,000, while the larger area designated as Hongqiao, covering
26 square kilometres, is home to 650,000 people. By 2020 the
population of the core will have tripled, while the wider area
will have almost doubled, to reach 1.2 million. To put this in
perspective, within the space of a decade, the new business area
will be built out to provide enough additional accommodation
for the entire population of the City of Glasgow. Or Dallas – or
the whole of Bahrain. Clearly, this demonstrates no shortage of
energy and ambition.

Low-carbon technologies and high-speed communication for a smart city are already de rigueur in Chinese cities. Shanghai already has twelve metro lines, five of which pass through the transport hub. Early reports of the content of Shanghai's 12th Five-Year Plan (FYP) indicate that IT infrastructure is a key priority. Shanghai's city mayor, Han Zheng, has pledged to invest 100 billion yuan (around £10 billion) in support of the city's key industries: IT, biotechnology, high-end equipment manufacturing, new energy, and the new materials sector.[1] The low-carbon city is already built into the Hongqiao CBD plan.[2] This is not, it should be noted, a green argument against growth, or an apologetic rationalisation for a lack of money, but instead stands as capital investment for the twenty-first century.

What was absent was any discussion about the involvement of the people who are and will be living there. This was not because the delegation had no concern for the population. Indeed, the whole idea is that the slogan of Shanghai Expo 2010 – 'Better City, Better Life' – will be realised through economic growth. One of the delegates commented: 'Of course construction companies can build in the core area where former residents have moved to a large residential district nearby.' So, while the overall population will increase, that will involve the displacement of the present residents and their replacement by a population geared to the central function of the new CBD: 'We expect the area will grow into a high-end innovation business center for the Yangtze Delta Region and that urban development of suburban Qingpu and Songjiang districts can be fostered as well.'[3] This incredible project does open up exciting commercial prospects. As one happy architecture company announced, having won a slice of the action:

The New Central Business District will be an energy efficient and environmentally conscious development characterized by its highly pedestrian-friendly environment. Located next to what will become the world's largest intermodal transit facility, the development will focus on reducing carbon dioxide emissions through a series of sustainable strategies, such as integration of highly efficient transportation systems, rain water collection and on-site water treatment, on-site renewable energy generation, and energy efficient building envelopes and systems.[4]

What was not part of the formula was the activity of the citizen. The citizen is but the passive recipient of a rather amazing plan. Since the urbanisation of China is acknowledged policy, considered the means of facilitating economic growth and social justice, the dynamism of the citizen has to find a release in conjunction with planning and economic dynamics.

CHINESE URBANISATION

The scale and dynamism of urban development in China are touchstones for the city in the new century. In 2008, for the first time in human history, more than 50 per cent of the global population lived in urban areas. China is moving rapidly towards the 50 per cent benchmark, after which urbanisation will continue. This is part of the largest and most significant movement of populations in human history. Around 15 million migrants arrived in the USA between 1881 and 1911, while around 300 million people have moved from rural to urban areas in China within a similar 30-year period. If China achieves an urbanisation rate of 50 per cent by 2040 (and this is the government target), then the shift of population will incorporate 500 million people. These are dizzying numbers.

The movement of population is a crucial component of the dynamism of Chinese cities. Migrant populations are by their nature dynamic. These are the people who have taken the risk, and grasped the opportunity, to move and seek a better life, often with their eyes set on future possibilities rather than present realities. It might be argued that this is less true when the scale of the movement is so vast, but the contemporary experience of Chinese cities testifies to the strength of both aspiration and dynamism.

Much more important than the sheer scale of this experience are its qualitative aspects – both actual and potential. The biggest cities of the future will not be in China. Although Beijing,

Shanghai and others are huge, they will not be as big as Dakar, Manila, Cairo and the megacities of the South. But size is not everything. The rapid urban population growth in many cities of the South does not follow the historically progressive model of urban development. Far from being built on surplus and the extension of the division of labour, it is instead associated with rural poverty and its relocation to urban disaster areas disconnected technically and socially from the pre-existing city.[5]

Chinese urban growth is explicitly based on economic surplus. This is not by any means to say that life for a migrant worker is easy; but it does represent a significant advance on the inexorable grind of peasant subsistence. Moreover, the ongoing network of social and economic relations between the newly arrived city-dweller and their village of origin consolidates the relationship between the two, serving to urbanise the countryside.[6]

In contrast to much contemporary urban growth elsewhere, and in line with Chinese urban policy, there will be many provincial and regional hubs alongside the great cities of the east coast. Chinese cities of 1 million and more will be numbered in the hundreds: each enough for a football team, a symphony orchestra, and the economies of scale that can make for the pleasures of a diverse and balanced urban environment.

In 2010 I visited the new city of Fang Cheng, in the previously less developed south-western province of Guangxi. Located on the Gulf of Tonkin, Fang Cheng is part of a regional development stretching from the coastal resort of Beihei in the east to the Vietnamese border in the west. The old port is being transformed in order to open the ASEAN countries to Chinese goods, while bringing ASEAN raw materials into China's western hinterland. Alongside the port, and linked to it by a bridge system, will be a new city, built around water and parkland, which within the space of the next decade will be home to a million people: double the current population. When the new migrants arrive from the rural hinterland, they will be freed not only from rural idiocy, but also from the need to travel the long distances to the eastern seaboard for the opportunities associated with urban life.

It is worth putting some facts about contemporary Chinese urban development into their historical context. For a start, urbanisation will mirror and advance upon the most sophisticated directions taken in the city regions of Tokyo–Osaka, the Boston–New York–Philadelphia nexus, and much of western Europe. These city regions are being replicated and surpassed in Beijing–Tianjin, Shanghai–Hangzhou–Nanjing, and the Pearl River Delta including Hong Kong. But there are also less well-known examples: Nanning–Beihei as part of China's aforementioned ASEAN strategy, Chongqing in the west, Shenyang–Dalian in the north, and so on.

Chinese urbanisation is a phenomenon for which the rather old-fashioned term 'uneven and combined development' is apt. But it is plausible, although not a given, that China's extraordinary economic dynamism will enable it to avoid the infrastructural and human costs of urban development associated with the rapid urban development of Europe and North America from the end of the eighteenth century. The Chinese model is spurred by the classical historical model of urbanity: a surplus inextricably linked to productive capacity. It is a beneficial and progressive model for global urban development.

Finally, the extent to which technical developments have mediated rather than a direct relationship with social change implies an extension of social possibilities and new sets of relationships between people. But, of course, there are no guarantees. As a simple example of the potential benefits, take the national high-speed rail network, which may open up a new relationship to space for millions of people. New forms and patterns of connectivity, however, do not guarantee the emergence of new content within the resulting new matrix of social relationships.

CONCEPTUALISING THE CITY

In May 2010 I attended a conference in Shanghai and listened to a highly respected specialist in urban planning explain that what the current discussion in China lacked was a sociological aspect. This might seem like a significant step in the right direction; but the role of sociological enquiry here was to integrate the citizen as a component part of the plan – a distinct but controllable factor. This represents not quite the engineering of souls, but, in the historic spirit of urban sociology, planning to adjust the responses of the citizen in alignment with the plan, intended to be in the best interests of both. This theorisation of the city, derived from both Chicago city planners[7] and the Chicago School of sociologists,[8] emphasises the positive benefits of planning in social control. The human ecology of cities is proving an attractive area for Chinese academics, since it allows the planner to retain the position of agent of progressive change, rather than ceding it to the less predictable citizen.

The mechanisms and processes through which this may be achieved are of great interest to Chinese policy-makers. One of these – economic growth – is immediately in their own hands. The second – social justice – is the element that eludes them, and for which they seek practical and technical answers, such as 'consultative procedures'.

Added to this, and in line with the two traditions of Chinese thought and Western sociology, is the urge and even the perceived responsibility to manipulate the environment in order to educate and improve the quality of citizens. The Chinese call this *suzhi* or 'population quality'.[9] It entails the idea that individuals carry with them a capacity and a responsibility to be good citizens. The word can be used in common speech, but it also refers to a central government initiative designed primarily to assign responsibility for poverty to individual behaviour rather than to the erosion of the national welfare system. The government, in turn, must find ways to encourage and inculcate good behaviour. Those without 'quality' must be educated, or trained, in citizenship.

The question of China's urban development has reinvigorated the perennial discussions associated with urban modernity and the impact on the people who live in it and through it. This is why I think it is worth exploring some of the nuances of how the city is described and conceptualised, not just in relation to its objective, built reality, but also to the subjective reading of the city through its impact on the hearts and minds of citizens.

The disruption of modernity – pre-eminently as enacted by the city – is the disruption of traditional hierarchies, customs, institutions and relationships. It can be exhilarating, and indeed liberatory; but it can also be confusing, worrying and alienating. At its heart, modernity is only a descriptive term for capitalist social relations. City life is the most important phenomenal form of this all-pervasive condition. It represents

> man's most successful attempt to remake the world he lives in more after his heart's desire. But, if the city is the world man created, it is the world in which he is henceforth condemned to live. Thus, indirectly, and without any clear sense of the nature of his task, in making the city man has remade himself.[10]

Urban life transforms human possibilities. By its very nature, it opens up not only the possibility of subjective interpretation of their environment, but an almost infinite range of ways of intervening with and transforming it objectively. These cannot be given, prefigured or ordained by the planned environment itself. The complexity of this relationship is illustrated in the following thought experiment:

> If a normal baby girl born 40,000 years ago were kidnapped by a time traveller and raised in a normal family in New York, she would be ready for college in 18 years ... Now, if I walk down New York's Fifth Avenue on an ordinary day, I will have within sight more human beings than most of those prehistoric hunter-gatherers saw in a lifetime.[11]

Of course, if the time traveller had 'landed' in many, too many, other contemporary environments – in sub-Saharan Africa, or the slums of Mumbai – then, even given the hard wiring of the human brain, her potential would not be realised. It is the *soft wiring* – the malleability of the human imagination (given sustenance and stimulation in a transformed and urban environment) – that unlocks genetic capacities. It is fashionable nowadays to characterise this as a good dose of social capital. However, human potential is more accurately understood as a result of fortunate positioning in the social division of labour. In China, the migrant worker from Yunnan, is, in a global sense, in just such a position. Her daughter may find she has more in common with a social-network friend in Seattle than with her cousin back in Yunnan. However, if the rural cousin were to move to the provincial capital Kunming, this would again change quite rapidly.

The new city-dweller can walk down Nanjing Road, in downtown Shanghai, like the time-traveller on Fifth Avenue, and see tens of thousands of people, but will never know, and will not need or want to know, more than a few of them. The direct encounters that characterise rural life are, for the most part, replaced by market transactions and bureaucratic relationships. The new city-dweller escapes the prying eyes of traditional and hierarchical societies, but at the same time becomes anonymous, and potentially isolated.

In objective historical terms, urban society erodes both the arbitrary incursion of nature into human society and the arbitrary power derived from inherited privilege. It promises – anonymously, like blind justice – both a level playing field, and, through the neutrality of rational decision-making institutions, boundless opportunity; a promise more easily met in the provision of traffic lights than in the wider allocation of society's resources.

In subjective terms, the individual, or group of citizens, has to negotiate not with a set of intimates with whom they have a personal relationship, however one-sided, but with an overarching and faceless bureaucratic apparatus. Since the apparatus applies a modus operandi which is abstract and distant, the individual citizen, whose life is concrete and immediate, may feel the need to subvert the plan. Moreover, in China, although the logic and rationality of the plan is inscribed in protocols and legislation, it is exercised through personal and often impenetrable networks.

From the standpoint of the planner, the question almost invariably takes the form of how, in a non-traditional environment, social control can be maintained in order to enhance the functioning, order and dynamics of the city? How can society be bound together, when at the core of capitalist social relations is a challenge to all traditional authority? The individual is not only 'free' in a market sense, but will immediately sense this potentiality in all other areas of civic life. How then can a measure of social order be preserved when the arbitrary use of force is no longer publicly acceptable, even in China?

Rational planning and public policy are products of modernity. They take the city as an objective, totalised entity, devised and moulded by rational purpose, employing a positivist methodology; and they presume that problems are susceptible to technical solutions. They are optimistic in outlook, ensuring that the traffic lights work and the trains run on time.

For the official sitting in the planning office, the priority is going to be the plan, as he seeks to give order to the activity of the city. If on the other hand you are a new migrant arriving in the city, you need a place to live and some form of paid work, whether on a building site or in your own small business; the licence to take up such work is a secondary consideration. This 'offence' to the plan and to regulation imparts to the city a distinctive texture, and registers positively in the city economy.

This spontaneous response to the external order of the city is often understood as the legacy of rural lifestyles and identities, and is described through an anthropological or ethnographic reading of the city. It is true, as casual observation confirms, that migrants live, at least initially, with other people coming from the same areas. Here familiarity, conferring a measure of trust, is the positive component of the intimate networks supplied by the prescribed family and status relations of rural society. But for trust to endure, and for it to be effective in the wider city environment, it would have to find a home – a source of legitimacy within the public policy process. This would, in turn, invest the public institution with authority. This is the peculiar, but not unique, problem for Chinese cities.

The two approaches to understanding the city, seemingly opposed, are in fact quite compatible. A top-down approach to planning can coexist peacefully with innumerable ethnographic studies of city life. The real difficulty arises when the city plan meets the irregular behaviour of the citizen, for this can be encompassed not by traffic-flow diagrams or participant observation, but only through public engagement.

THE CENTRAL RELATIONSHIP

The mutual interaction between a globalised economy, cultural diversity and human artefacts gives rise to urbanisation, the sociology of the city, and the making of public policy as the relationship between the state, the market and the citizen. This is not a linear or one-dimensional relationship because it applies simultaneously at global, national and local levels. It also applies differentially to different groups of people. Furthermore, each component of the triangle relates in two directions (see Figure 1.1), and, as we have already seen, can be understood through the further interaction of our positivist and ethnographic models.

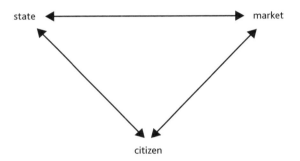

Figure 1.1   The simple relationship

This last point can be approached through an important variation on this relationship (see Figure 1.2). In this modification, there is still a negotiation between state and market, which I shall refer to as 'planned space'. This derives from the institutional authority for large developments. It can be beneficial and well-organised, or harmful and corrupt, or take one of many positions between those two poles.

I term the relationship between the citizen and the market 'lived space' – an expression of the informal economy, or small-scale entrepreneurship, or even the daily routine of millions of people: this includes public transport, street vending and protection rackets.

Figure 1.2   An important variation on this relationship

Both conceptions of space, which in fact cannot be separated except for the purpose of logical clarity, themselves redefine cultural orientations towards a place. The city is not mere space, but the sum total of the actions of the people in it. It may be useful to give a provisional summary of how this might apply to urbanisation, public policy and life in the city – a city such as Shanghai.

EXPO 2010: BETTER CITY, BETTER LIFE

Everyone knows the formula: London, the dominant city of the nineteenth century; New York, the pre-eminent city of the twentieth century; and, Shanghai, the city of the twenty-first century. The ambition expressed by Shanghai – by which I mean that of its municipal government, as directed by the national State Council – to be the key global city, is a fair bet to be realised. It might happen in a much more profound way than for other cities in the past, or in the presently existing global cities, to both of which categories New York and London belong. This is because Shanghai's global nature corresponds not only to its economic dynamism – a feature it shares with historic precursors – but also to the possibility of a much more profound cultural diversity than in contemporary New York and London (even if such diversity remains underdeveloped).

Shanghai takes its place in a world which is far more interconnected than in the past. This interconnection manifests itself in straightforward ways for an international elite that moves seamlessly between cities – but in more subtle and ambivalent ways for those of its residents who are still defined by their place of residence and by the space of the city itself. This is an example of asymmetrical cosmopolitanism. Shanghai is a global city with increasing cultural diversity and a growing capacity to define new styles, but these things are experienced differentially by its constituent population.[12] The street vendor may be more cosmopolitan than the city official by virtue of having a more varied interaction between the global and the local. The vendor, after all, has a much wider variety of encounters and experiences, but these tend to be reactive and intuitive responses (intercontinental commuting is unnecessary when you live in the economic hub of the world) to a global dynamic over which he or she has little control.

The dynamic economic development of Shanghai means that the government can put train stations, housing and employment all in the same place, or at least plan to do so. Shanghai has more skyscrapers than New York, and a public transport system bigger than London's. It is already the centre of a regional hub in the Yangtze Delta that includes significant cities, such as Hangzhou and even Nanjing. Its 12 per cent economic growth rate easily exceeds that of China as a whole. Per capita income, at $125 per year in the 1950s, has been accelerating since the 1970s, reaching $6,000 in 2005. This was all to be showcased at Shanghai Expo 2010. The Expo site was at the heart of the urban redevelopment of both the city region as a whole and of the city's core. It was identified as a key component of the greening of the old industrial areas along the Huangpu River. All of this could be seen in a scale model the size of a basketball court on public display in downtown Shanghai. This model was proudly viewed by local people as well as visiting dignitaries, but it does not translate directly into the trust and legitimacy that would give the city a much more powerful and profound momentum.

Shanghai Expo 2010 offers an interesting example of how Chinese planners understand urbanisation, how they hope to intervene in the lives of the residents, and how some residents have responded. It is a good example of planned space that is more ambivalent than transport links and new housing. Transport and planning could be categorised as products of efficient corruption: economic dynamism, state resources, large profits for developers, facilities for the population.

On my previous visits to Shanghai, I had become intrigued at the rationale for the Expo. Over the course of 12 months (before and during the Expo), I carried out a survey with around 80 respondents: volunteers, citizens and civil servants. I also conducted detailed interviews with leading policy-makers and planners, a workshop with Shanghai students, and street interviews around Shanghai.

On one Saturday, I travelled by metro 45 minutes from Renmin Square, with one change at the Maglev intersection, to the Pudong suburbs to interview people who had been moved in order to accommodate the huge Expo site in the centre of the city. It was a clean, efficient and pleasant enough journey. Across the road was a four-storey shopping mall – although it was laid out more like an internal open market, with open stalls rather than individual retail outlets. There were no buses to residential areas, but a teeming mass of bicycle-driven taxis: illegal but necessary.

The taxis reminded me of a story from the *Shanghai Daily* about the entrapment of ordinary motorists by teams employed by the municipality to catch non-licensed taxis. The article reported that the licensing squads had been caught hailing motorists and asking for a lift to the hospital. Money was then thrown down before the passenger leapt out of the vehicle, and then going on to prosecute the motorist for illegally touting for rides. This is inefficient corruption. A simpler solution might be to provide buses and register more taxis.

Each line of apartments was about 100 metres long, stretching into the distance, like the lines of terraces of England's northern industrial towns: neat, two storey blocks, of about the standard of the early seventies in the UK.

At first we met only older residents, sitting in small groups in the shade. They did not like the new environment: no small shops or cafés, longer distances to schools and clinics. They were right about the immediate environment. It was comfortable but bare. But after an hour or so we started to meet a wider range of residents: a youth who came from downtown to spend time with his grandparents and who was oblivious to the distance; a late-middle-aged couple pleased with the resettlement money, who used a subsidised bus to get back into the city. More intriguingly, we met a young woman from Dalian who had secured a technical job in a nearby German-owned chemical factory. She had managed to rent one of the relocation apartments. The doctor who owned her apartment had rented out his place immediately and moved back to the city centre.

The plan had produced the metro line, and reasonable housing. The people had already started to fill in the gaps, and at the same time the global economy of Shanghai was being supplemented by entrepreneurial activity of many sorts. This seemed to work reasonably well, so my first question to the planners was: Why Expo? To which the inevitable first response was that it would help to build up the infrastructure. The more senior of them were able to confirm that this was an integral part of the 11th Five-Year Plan. In response to my suggestion that the Shanghai government seemed perfectly capable of building an effective city infrastructure without resorting to such a major demand on resources as an Expo, the planners argued that the pressure of the deadline and the scale of the enterprise would stimulate the human resource capabilities of the thousands of administrative and technical experts involved in the planning and execution of Expo.

Moreover, the fact that an Expo could be successfully achieved would signal that Shanghai had already arrived as a global city. The oft-repeated mantra was: 'Let the Chinese see the world; and the world see China.' But this was often only the preamble to a much more telling explanation. Expo 2010 was, as both the planners and the volunteers insisted, a powerful instrument for educating the citizen. The argument was that the Shanghainese had to be moulded into acceptable inhabitants of a new global city.

Unsurprisingly, this particular response was almost entirely absent in the interviews with ordinary citizens – they did not report a need to be moulded into acceptable citizens; but it was pervasive in the volunteer response. It is clear that this rubric was a significant element in volunteer training. This is a well-tried technique in professional and vocational training: instil the appropriate attitudes in a new cohort at their entry

point, and they will then transmit the new culture to a wider
audience. In this reading, the purpose of Expo is to transform
the social ambience: to civilise the city itself through the pressure
of international exposure.

But it is far from clear how much of an impact – let alone a
long-term effect – this may have. In autumn 2009, a municipal
campaign was launched to end the local habit of wearing
pyjamas to the shops. Young volunteers were primed to berate
people with the lines: 'Dear auntie, do you think it reflects well
on our city to go outside in your pyjamas?' But with the shops
on your doorstep, it's a reasonable habit. More importantly,
pyjamas were actually worn as a status symbol, demonstrating
that the wearer could afford unique sleepwear! The campaign
thus had little impact.

For most of my interviewees, at least, Expo was a disappointing
experience: it was hard work, the whole event was not of the
quality they had expected, and in the end they would return to
being unemployed graduates.

Shanghai was the key centre of China's first encounter with
modernity, in the inter-war period. During the Maoist period,
this emblematic city of China's first modernity was stigmatised.
The aim was to endorse the prevailing ethos of promoting the
petty industrialisation of rural areas in a perverse, inverted
elimination of the gap between town and country.[13] In the
inter-war period Shanghai was already a city of international
significance, in terms both of its size and economic development,
and of its social energy and cultural production.[14] This legacy
of intellectual endeavour, social liberalism and political action
was what made it so alarming to the regime after 1949. This
experiment in urban living in the 1920s and 1930s, has yet to
be reproduced in contemporary Shanghai. Although the material
requisites are there in abundance – along with the undisputed
energy, aspiration and independent spirit of its population – there
remains an absence at the centre of the city consisting of more
than just the deserted Expo site.

After a period of 40 years in which Shanghai ceased to be a city
of migrants, it is now returning to its historic position as both
a centre for internal migration and a global centre. Shanghai is

destined to be a global city, but it is still also a 'locality' for the majority of its population – even, perhaps especially, for the ones who only arrived a week ago.

The urban planner often works on a grand scale, but the resident – and potential citizen – views the world from the vantage point of the particular. There are a variety of locations where the two might come together. The archetypal meeting place might be just such a location: park, shopping centre or theatre. An institution such as a health centre or town hall, or even an idea, instrumental need, or conception of public good – all might provide such an opportunity

In Shanghai there is a continuous mediation between the global and the local, but little between the government planner and the city-dweller. The planner thus provides anaemic versions of what he perceives the international visitor to want – the turgid bar district of Xintiandi, 'The City's Living Room', superimposed on the old and distinctive *shikumen* architecture – while the city changes behind his back.

In the course of the city's growth and transformation, both in the experience of the citizen and in the organisation of space, there emerge new boundaries and new definitions of public and private space, or non-space: shopping malls, airport lounges, gated communities, office complexes, heritage sites. Excluding some people from certain places is intended to elevate the city in the pecking order of global cities. This may be a result, but it certainly inhibits the texture and vitality of the city.

In tension with bounded space and asymmetrical cosmopolitanism is the injunction or aspiration of the Right to the City.[15] The assumption of the liberatory moment of urbanisation, as a challenge to traditional custom and hierarchy, is that the city is a book open to all.

As the focus of planning attention turns to the CBD's transport links and the Gucci outlets on the revamped Bund, we should keep an eye on developments on the Expo site. I was unable to elicit an answer from policy-makers as to what was planned for such a prestigious area, beyond the scheme to keep four permanent pavilions and demolish most of the rest. There is a lot of money to be made in property development, but more international hotels and conference centres will demand a lot of street activity to keep Shanghai on track to become the emblematic city of the twenty-first century, rather than – as a friend described it to me over a beer on his first visit – Croydon on acid.

NOTES

1. 'Industrial Policy in China and the 12th Five Year Plan (2011–2015)', *China Analytics*, 12 October 2010.
2. Yang Wenyao, 'Practice and Innovation of Low-Carbon Concept in the Planning of Hongqiao Business District', 46th ISOCARP Congress, 2010.
3. Speech given by Wang Zhongwei, head of the publicity department of CPC Shanghai, 16 September 2009.
4. Project data, Skidmore, Owings & Merrill, 'Hongqiao New CBD, Shanghai, China', at <som.com>.
5. Mike Davies, *Planet of Slums*, Verso, 2006.
6. Doug Saunders, *Arrival City: How the Largest Migration in History is Reshaping Our World*, Heinemann, 2010, pp. 22–4.
7. Alan Hudson, 'Mr Science and Mr Democracy: The Pursuit of Modernity in China', *City* 12: 2 (July 2008), pp. 161–70.
8. Ibid.
9. Rachel Murphy, 'Turning Peasants into Modern Chinese Citizens: "Population Quality" Discourse, Demographic Transition and Primary Education', *China Quarterly*, March 2004, pp. 1–20.
10. Robert Park, *On Social Control and Collective Behaviour*, University of Chicago Press, 1967.
11. Kwame Anthony Appiah, *Cosmopolitanism: Ethics in a World of Strangers*, Allen Lane, 2006.
12. Robin Visser, *Cities Surround the Countryside: Urban Aesthetics in Post-Socialist China*, Duke University Press, 2010. pp 118–20.
13. Rana Mitter, *Modern China: A Very Short Introduction*, Oxford University Press, 2008.

14. Rana Mitter, *A Bitter Revolution: China's Struggle with the Modern World*, Oxford University Press, 2005.

15. Henri Lefebvre, 'The Right to the City', in Lefebvre, *Writings on Cities*, ed. and transl. E. Kofman and E. Lebas, Blackwell, 1996 [1968], pp. 63–184.

2
The Emerging City
Africa's Metropolitan Mindset

Alastair Donald

[London is] immense without being immediately impressive, tolerant without any permanent preferences, attracting increasing specimens of the best of all earthly things without being susceptible to any perceptible improvement.
Ford Madox Ford, 'The Soul of London'

Humanity is on the move. In what will become the largest migration in history, by the middle of this century, 2 billion or perhaps 3 billion people can be expected to reject the prospect of confinement to a life of rural immiseration. Instead they will opt for the potential freedoms of the city – for the chance to pursue dreams and realise ambitions for a better life.[1]

It is the break-neck pace of urbanisation in Asia and Africa which means that, by 2050, humanity will be a largely urban species.[2] From the late eighteenth century, the masses made their way across the land and over the oceans to the emerging cities of London, Paris and New York; yet by the time Europe and the New World were largely urbanised, more than two-thirds of the world's people remained stranded in rural isolation. By the beginning of this century, the towers of São Paulo, the *barrios* of Bogotá and the motorway networks of Santiago had signalled that the people of Latin America were also largely urban-based. Yet the majority of the global populace remained outside metropolitan centres.

Step forward Istanbul, Lagos, Jakarta, Chongqing – and Qingdao, Kinshasa, Klang Valley and Khartoum. More than 1 million people a week currently swell the population of the world's emerging cities – the equivalent to building a new

Bangkok every couple of months.[3] In India, by 2026, around 14 Delhis or 18 Bombays or 30 Bangalores will be needed,[4] while in China the number of cities has soared in the last 30 years from 193 to 640, with 300 more planned. And there are novel typologies too: 'mega-cities', 'meta-cities' and 'hypercities', while by 2025, China will have 15 'supercities'[5] – each accommodating 25 million people or more; then there are supersized urban corridors, agglomerations of industrial centres such as India's 1,500km stretch between Jawaharlal Nehru Port (in Navi Mumbai) to Dadri and Tughlakabad (in Delhi).[6]

But emerging cities should not be reduced to stories of bricks and mortar, or tales woven around demography and statistics. The United Nations' influential *State of the World's Cities* report cautioned that '[c]ities contain both order and chaos. In them reside beauty and ugliness, virtue and vice … Cities are the physical manifestation of humanity's noblest ideas, ambitions and aspirations, but when not planned or governed properly, can be the repository of society's ills.'[7] This description accepts – and perhaps endorses – the existence of opposites in the city. After all, creative tensions have always been central to the metropolitan experience.

Yet as Africa usurps Asia as the most rapidly urbanising region in the world, the discussion has become laced with anxiety. Commentaries often start by stressing that cities are human creations, designed to meet our needs and aspirations.[8] For many, however, the emerging cities of the twenty-first century will contribute little to a flourishing civilisation, but instead mark the return of the City of the Dreadful Night,[9] only this time simmering in a hellish sub-Saharan heat. 'Is Urbanisation in Africa Pathological?' asks the UN, fearing not only the return of Dickensian urban decay, but the reinforcing of contemporary corrosive forces of social exclusion and intolerance. Many analysts, it notes, now view urbanisation in Africa through a prism of 'abnormality'. Slums in Nairobi, Lagos and other African cities have contributed to a sense that the continent's rapid urban growth makes it 'dysfunctional'.[10]

But if, as is alleged, the emerging city is a slough of despond, why have so many continued to make it their home? No doubt conditions are appalling for millions. But, casting a glance back at Victorian Britain, was the influx of rural poor into the hovels of London not also a case of squalid repression? Is this not history in the making, in all its messy complexity? And if so, should we not accept this as part and parcel of the process of creating the future? On the other hand, we might also justifiably ask: Should we have to suffer in order to thrive? Must there still be rites of passage for the twenty-first century urban migrant?

Focusing primarily on nineteenth-century London and twenty-first-century Nairobi, this chapter looks at some of the uncomfortable realities of urban emergence, and asks whether there is anything natural – or passive – about the conditions in emergent cities.

LONDON: THE CITY ILLIMITABLE

The most striking feature of London at the end of the nineteenth century was its modernity.[11] From 1850 until 1900, 'trying your luck' in the dazzle and glitter of London drew between 30,000 and 50,000 people into the city every single year. Of course, many viewed the bright lights from the distant hovels of Paddington or Deptford. But that wasn't the point. The city was on the move and was something to be part of – a stepping stone to a bigger, brighter, better future, in a city that – in the imagination, at least – could stimulate and satisfy every appetite, whether of businessman or beggar, of artist or labourer.

Much has been written about modern London, but few captured it better than Ford Madox Ford in *The Soul of London*, an impressionistic portrait of the Edwardian city.[12] By then, the city of Engels and Dickens, densely packed and barely five miles across, had burst out into the countryside, an assemblage of homes, commerce and industry spread across the lower Thames basin. The endlessly shifting scenes and impressions – fragmented, bewildering in their variety – captures the modern city rendered through the artist's imagination. They represent a journey of discovery about the nature of a modern city, and the way people come to terms with their new lives.

This is a modern London that conflicts – uproariously – with most current ideas about what a city should be. In contrast to current cautious injunctions to know our limits, slow down, take care, avoid strangers, and mind our manners, to be Modern was to experience personal and social life as a maelstrom, to find one's world and oneself in perpetual disintegration and renewal, trouble and anguish, ambiguity and contradiction.[13] Dreams were pursued, and hopes frequently dashed. But life offered possibilities, and a sense that previous constraints could be thrown off.

The Modern city thereby made a mockery of the 'sensible rule of thumb' used by the Administrative Council in its attempt to demarcate city life into a series of localities. Such anti-metropolitan attitudes are reminiscent of more recent attempts to promote the 'urban village' as a means to tame the expansive nature of metropolitan life by promoting local communities. Instead, and in a celebration of urban migrants freeing themselves from the stultifying atmosphere and suffocating customs of the village, to be Modern was, as far as possible, to experience life without boundaries, to resist the need to engage in a constant quest for definition: 'England is a small country. The world is infinitesimal amongst the planets. But London is illimitable'.[14]

A psychological city without boundaries is also, however, a perturbing place of impersonality and loneliness as well as opportunity. 'London is the world town, not because of its vastness; it is vast because of its assimilative powers', says Madox Ford,[15] recognising that it was not so much its physical size as its energy that drew people in. But if newcomers are ingested and energised, they are also stripped of existing comforts and familiar traits. Life in a disorientating world of impermanence can frequently be solitary and anonymous, unsettling, fragmentary and despairing.

From an individual perspective, even though it might not always have been experienced in such a positive way, it was still a liberation: an environment and an emerging set of social relations that brought with them the possibility of freedom from many of the ties and rituals that previously held people back. Yes, there was dirt and squalor; poverty was frequently extreme;

and you probably didn't know your neighbours. But ultimately, all of these might be considered prices worth paying. As places where new social interactions were being forged on the basis of the destruction of traditional relations, emerging cities offered the individual the potential to have a say in his or her own future.

Where provincial life was still and mundane, in the city it pulsed with individual ambitions and communal passions. Those seeking adventure could revel – and struggle – in a new interconnectedness of human experience. This was the birth of a metropolitan mindset, shaped around the need to be assertive and demanding; in the bar, the workplace and the streets, life became more demonstrative and theatrical, wits needed sharpening lest you be taken advantage of, humour became a means of both defence and attack, and the articulation of crass generalisations carried the risk of ridicule – as the 'know-nothing' out-of-towner.

Indeed, questions that in the past might have had a set of predetermined, formulaic answers now demanded more considered and active responses: individual judgement was required as to what mattered and what didn't; as to right and wrong; and as to how interests could be maximised either by the individual or, increasingly, by a collective body. Such was the acceptance of city life – but not fate. This was the emergence of cities as places of creative engagement, not in the Richard Florida sense, but in terms of the development of the human subject. That they were in a dialectical relationship with the city is true, but humans were stepping into the driving seat.

NAIROBI: THE TRANSIENT CITY

One degree south of the equator and a mile above sea level, the Kenyan capital Nairobi only acquired city status in 1950. What was then the small commercial and business hub of the British East Africa protectorate is today a metropolitan region of 6 million people. By 2030 that figure might double.[16] Many aspects of the city do not distinguish it from most modern cities in the South: traffic crawling along outdated infrastructure; a lively commercial centre; dusty, bustling urban neighbourhoods. The spacious suburbs of colonial times remain. More surprisingly, the growth of recent years has not obliterated the greenery or forests that have been retained within the cityscape.

But in the contemporary discussion of Nairobi, any strides it has taken towards the modern world lie buried beneath a view of the city as little more than a collection of fetid, densely packed slums; mega-cities such as Nairobi are, says one critic, 'stinking mountains of shit that would appal even the most hardened of Victorians'.[17] The city that formed at the heart of the east African region, where human life is said to have begun, has become a central focus of the fears over where it might be headed.

So is this a uniquely horrific urban phenomenon in the making? Given Nairobi's new reputation, the city and its slums have encouraged considerable interest, as agencies and assorted visitors descend to inspect or respect the natives, to map or highlight the plight of those living in these apparent disaster zones. There are more than 200 'informal settlements' within the city boundaries, but as they are not formally recognised, they lack services such as running water and electricity.[18] Open sewers and garbage mountains are all too common. According to the United Nations, over 1.5 million people live in densely packed mud huts or tin sheds crammed into a tight space that represents only 5 per cent of the city's residential land.[19] In fact these figures are likely to be considerably exaggerated by the various agencies working in the city. In the absence of authoritative data, some reports have suggested that population figures were 'entirely made up to suit the interests of particular groups'.[20]

Of all Nairobi's slums, the most 'famous' and largest is Kibera, which consists of nine 'villages' lying a mere four miles west of the urban core. Someone who has spent more time in Kibera than most visitors is the journalist Robert Neuwirth, who became interested in the 'squatter neighbourhoods' of what he calls 'shadow cities'.[21] Neuwirth's account is useful because he offers some practical insights into slum life. But it also exposes some of the more problematic ideas at the heart of the western commentary on emerging cities.

In Neuwirth's *Shadow Cities*, the reader is taken on a tour around the 'stagnant swollen valley' that is the location for the 'mud hut metropolis' of Kibera. In some ways it is not for the fainthearted. Flies, pigs and effluent surround mud blockhouses ventilated by one-foot-wide alleys strewn with refuse; there are the overflowing sewers and latrines in the rainy season, the thieves who knock holes in huts and empty the contents, and the gang violence that can descend after dark.[22] Yet this description seems less like a unique picture of Kibera than a reminder of slums throughout the ages – of Victorian London, for example, where 60 people might occupy just a four-room house.[23] There, the rookery of St Giles – a 'thieves' quarter' – prompted one famous visitor to suggest that it amounted to a neighbourhood of filth and tottering ruin that surpassed description, where heaps of garbage and ashes were strewn in all directions, and where foul liquids emptied before the doors gathered in stinking pools.[24] None of which is intended to excuse conditions in Kibera, which are an affront to the twenty-first century. Nevertheless, slums are not an historically unusual element in the emergence of cities.

In defiance of many one-dimensional portraits of poverty and people down on their luck, it is clear from Neuwirth's account that slums such as Kibera are home to a diverse collection of characters. There are the entire families who live in a single room, but also the anonymous millionaire property tycoons extorting unfeasibly high rents. We meet City Council clerks and the members of 'merry–go-rounds' – neighbourhood networks in which people pool their resources to get by; water-sales profiteers and the women forced to haul water home from communal taps. Unsurprisingly, residents have aspirations for better roads and decent healthcare; but there are already vibrant social establishments such as the Western Motel, which, with a bit of decoration and a fridge, would not be out of place anywhere in Europe.[25]

Neuwirth goes too far when he rejects the term 'slum' as loaded with the 'emotional judgement' of outsiders.[26] He has a romanticised view of squatters. Nevertheless, he is right to talk up the determination, resourcefulness and resilience that slum-dwellers exhibit when confronting daunting circumstances. Whatever the problems of daily life, they mostly exhibit a steely determination to present themselves clearly as a force to be reckoned with – as people with a history documented in photographs, who support families and make their way in the world. And this is not an endless present, but the beginning of the future, of moving onto something better: they are '[n]ot idlers, but wage earners. Not ignorant, but educated. Not humdrum, but people with a career, a business, a calling, a vocation.'[27]

Investigating 'arrival cities',[28] the urban spaces around the world that accommodate migrants, the journalist Doug Saunders also visited Kibera, and he too confounded many of the assumptions about slum-dwellers. Families in slums, like millions before them, move to cities because doing so represents the best hope of changing their lives. Not surprisingly, a slum seems like a fair prospect when a single meal of porridge and a bed in a grass hut is the return for an exhausting day farming maize and potatoes. Suffocating customs, religious duties, restrictive dress codes and enforced marriage provide every reason to escape.[29]

The determined spirit of adventure that drives those who escape rural life also serves them well on arrival. Despite appalling, unsanitary conditions, poverty-line wages, difficulty paying school fees, and periodic descents into violence, a resilient response to problems is typical: 'The only way I'll return to the village is in a casket', says one migrant. Typical too is the appreciation of the potential freedoms of the city: 'I am a Nairobi resident now, I speak the language, I know how to be a women here.' Some might call this naively optimistic, but given the tendency – in western society at least – to accept your lot fatalistically, this is a potent reminder that cities can be, should be, places where identities are shed. You are not what you are born with; life is a matter for urban-centred negotiation, possible precisely because of the concentration of urban humanity. Things are made to change, by force of both will and numbers.

Whether in Nairobi or Bombay or Cairo, similar dreams of improvement abound. Upon their arrival, slum-dwellers are already planning their escape – envisaging how future wages will fund the move to a better neighbourhood, maybe a new city, or even an entirely new continent. Emerging cities thus have a universal appeal: discomfort in the city (for a villager) is an investment in a better future; people are a 'collection of transients, on their way from somewhere to somewhere else'.[30]

THE URBAN EMERGENCE

What shines through in accounts of life in slums is an incredible sense of energy, noise and bustle: jitneys hauling people and goods; ever-busy tailors, carpenters, potters, cooks, bar workers; goods hawked and haggled over in local shops or markets; recyclers churning through waste, discarded goods or engine parts. Busy people, high densities, lots of interaction: in these images of local hives of activity, it is not difficult to recognise the ideals of western *urbanistas*. Urban village champion and 'slumdog millionheir'[31] Prince Charles asserts for example, that on entering a slum, 'what looks from the outside like an immense mound of plastic and rubbish' in fact contains 'an intricate network of streets with miniature shops, houses and workshops, each one made out of any material that comes to hand'.[32]

What are celebrated as 'intricate networks' are actually better understood as communities that, to a greater or lesser extent, are disconnected economically and socially from the more dynamic aspects of city life. Low-paid casual employment reflects the absence of jobs in industrial parks; the buying of local goods reflects the failure to develop well-stocked supermarkets. But instead of recognising informal networks as merely survival mechanisms – temporary measures that might build enough momentum to move on – they are frequently idealised by western observers as a type of lifestyle choice.

Historically, emerging cities such as London thrived not just on the urban energy supplied by migrants, but through the dynamic growth of industry, commerce and markets. Friedrich Engels wrote in 1844 that 'London, where a man may wander for hours together without reaching the beginning of the end … is a strange thing',[33] and went on to record the condition of the working classes in London, Manchester and elsewhere. In his introduction to a recent edition of that famous work, the historian Tristram Hunt emphasises that Engels illustrates the inhumanity of capitalism and demonstrates its social injustices.[34] But in his eagerness to legitimise his own distaste for 'unfettered markets', Hunt ends up downplaying the huge benefits, of the 'colossal centralisation' of modernising London: 'Heaping together of two and a half millions of human beings at one point', Engels noted, has 'multiplied the power of this two and a half millions a hundredfold; has raised London to the commercial capital of the world, created the giant docks and assembled the thousand vessels that continually cover the Thames.'[35]

After Kenya gained independence in 1963, a decade of sharp growth boosted Nairobi's chances of escaping from underdevelopment. New industries – such as plastic and metals processing, vehicle assembly, and the food and chemical industries – grew alongside a new urban infrastructure. It is true that not all new migrants were absorbed into this modernising process, and the city failed to develop enough momentum to stop the growth of slums. But whatever its problems, Nairobi was being shaped by distinctly modernising forces.

By the early 1970s, fears over population growth and environmental damage started to influence the outlook and policies of the World Bank and other western institutions, which were influential in shaping the future of the developing world. Support for ambitious growth and industrialisation was no longer the priority for western institutions directing investment in the developing world, and urbanisation too came to be viewed less favourably.[36] As Michael Owens explains in Chapter 4 of the present volume, from the 1970s onwards the ambitious urban planning projects that were such a prominent feature of post-war development in western cities and newly independent African countries started to fall from favour.

The policies shaping development in Kenya and other African countries from the early 1970s onwards contrast starkly with the more strident attitudes to development exhibited by Victorian entrepreneurs. In Nairobi, even before the new scepticism towards growth was formalised in policy terms, Kenyan President Jomo Kenyatta had been warned by one influential western figure that 'freedom had become too much connected with a free-for-all, with land grabs and general breakdown of responsibility'.[37] This is in vivid contrast to the confidence that shaped the emergence of Victorian cities. Then, land grabs were seen less as a problem than as something to aspire to. Not only were factories and the power of industry a cause for celebration, but Victorian capitalists took an almost giddy pleasure in the desecration of the countryside for urban development. Factories planted on fields, rivers diverted, forests cut down – all were favourable signs of progress.[38]

The reaction against industrialisation and urbanisation in developing countries led to a significant change in how Nairobi developed. Instead of investment being made available for new industry, motorways and modern housing – the types of development that could spur growth and help overcome poverty and the escalation of slums – it was instead diverted into support for agriculture and rural services. Rather than underwriting ambitious plans for growth, the bar was set merely at alleviating the worst manifestations of poverty.[39] This did little to stop rural-to-urban migration: for reasons already explained, people continued to view the city as more attractive than the impoverished countryside. But without the means to invest in urban advancement and modernisation, more slums and informal economies were the inevitable outcome.

While in the 1970s and 1980s urbanisation tended to be viewed as a problem, the distinctive feature of the past decade or so has been that cities have come back into favour, most especially among the very Western agencies and urban theorists who in the past were most suspicious.[40] Behind this Damascene conversion to support for urbanisation, it is important to note that the concerns fuelling the original hostility to cities remain firmly in place. But while fears over population growth, resource use and urban freedoms show no signs of subsiding, cities, according to received wisdom, are now the best hope of containing the damage. The new-found support for urbanisation does not signal the return of an ambitious commitment to growth, industrialisation and modernisation. In fact, quite the opposite. The prospect that the Nairobis of this world might acquire western standards of living and mobility seems horrifying to many, and reflects the absence of a modernising zeal among western elites.

Today, the fashionable agenda is for prosperity *without* growth.[41] Consequently, life in emerging cities – at least in the less dynamic economies of the South – is often experienced as the absence of modernisation. An additional problem is that, in the contemporary West, it is modernisation that stands condemned as the source of Africa's problems – a symbol not of dynamism, but of a loss of control over the future.

THE ANTI-MODERNIST IMAGINATION

Today, acceptance of urbanisation *without* modernisation reflects diminished support for the progressive ambition for material progress that could help wipe slums from the face of the earth. One consequence is that slums have recently become something to accept, defend, and sometimes even celebrate. Not many are as openly enthusiastic as eco-pragmatist Stewart Brand, who argues that we should 'save the slums'[42] because they in turn can save the planet.[43] Nevertheless, over recent years there has been an increasing willingness to accept the presence of slums and to argue, for example, that those living in slums are in need of rights, as opposed to new homes. One outcome of this trend has been an emphasis on slum upgrading, rather than on demolition accompanied by the building of new homes.

The idea of slum upgrading[44] emerged in the 1970s, when, after rejecting support for large-scale urbanisation, pragmatists at the World Bank and UN-HABITAT latched on to the self-help ideas of English anarchist John Turner – an enthusiast for emergent settlements based on self-build and small-scale incremental improvements. Western agencies, as well as both their radical and conservative critics, generally operate today on the basis of agreement 'not to eradicate these communities but to stop treating them as slums … and start treating them as neighbourhoods to be improved'.[45] Slums are said to benefit from the 'order and harmony' associated with self-organising, complex systems, while modernisation is decried for its 'fragmented, deconstructed housing estates'.[46]

As we argue elsewhere in this book, if modern infrastructure and affordable housing are provided, people seem to adapt. Today's defenders of slums and of self-organising networks have the problem the wrong way round. The modern city does not suffer from the lack of 'self-organising' emergent properties; it has simply moved on to something better. Large-scale modern urban networks are the result of learning to employ planning, design and large-scale construction techniques to move beyond the limitations of local networks. The universalising dynamic of access across the city integrates the different functional elements. If modern development fails, that failure often reflects not the housing or industrial zones themselves, but the lack of modern infrastructure to connect them into the large-scale networks of the twenty-first-century city.

When slum-dwellers do refuse the move to new modern apartments, their motives are often misinterpreted. Rather than being understood as a sign that they are holding out for something better, a refusal to move is taken as an indication that people want to stay in slum communities. The existence of slums is even celebrated as an act of resistance to the perceived excesses of modernity and global capitalism: slum-dwellers 'commit treason by being there, and they show that this little place isn't like anywhere else in the world'.[47] Expressing a sentiment that Prince Charles would no doubt welcome, squatters, it has been said, 'offer a different way of looking at the land [and] live by a more ancient notion: the idea that every person has a natural right, simply by being born'.[48] This turns on its head the key aspirations behind migration to cities. Its aim was not to create a new urban parochialism, but to transcend the realm of pre-ordained privilege. Whatever the undoubted difficulties of being thrust into a modernising world, the great benefit was that of being liberated from 'natural rights', as all the morals and customs of the 'good old times' were obliterated.

While some have romanticised slums, others, such as urban theorist Mike Davis, author of *Planet of Slums*, paint a much bleaker picture.[49] Rather than recognising the restless energy of places operating as a stepping stone to a better future, Davis is chief proselytiser of the slum apocalypse. His premise is that

policy think-tanks and international relations institutes have
suffered a failure of imagination when it comes to anticipating the
implications of catastrophic overcrowding and under-provision.
By painting a picture of potentially apocalyptic consequences,
Davis seeks to provide a wake-up call, pointing the finger at the
middle classes who he says are bunkered in electrified security
villages, having relinquished all moral and cultural insight into
the badlands outside.

Yet, for all that it sets itself up as a radical critique – of
neoliberals, of western institutions, of slum apologists – this
vision of the slum apocalypse is underpinned by the same
disillusion with modernity evident in many of those on the sharp
end of his barbed criticisms. From cyber-modernity' to 'pirate
urbanisation' to 'pathologies of urban form', Davis uses a huge
range of barely intelligible labels for emerging cities, many of
which appear to express his extreme disillusion with the modern
world. For example, 'new and entirely artificial hazards' are
said to result from poverty's interaction with toxic industries,
anarchic traffic and collapsing infrastructures. This vision of the
city as savaged by modernity, disconnected from civilisation and
beyond human control recalls the views of Oswald Spengler, who
saw the city as the determinative form of a culture, and linked
the decline of western civilisation with the rise of modernity.

It is not too far-fetched to suggest that Spengler's description
of 'cities laid out for ten to twenty million inhabitants,
spread over enormous areas of countryside [with] traffic and
communications that we should regard as fantastic to the point
of madness' would sit comfortably in *Planet of Slums*. Likewise,
when Davis is critical of urban development that cuts fisherman
off from the sea, undermining a life lived symbiotically with
nature,[50] he seems to echo longstanding fears that the city
is a misguided attempt to dominate forces that are beyond
our control, marking the end of 'organic growth' and the
beginning of 'an inorganic and therefore unrestrained process
of agglomerations'.[51]

All things considered, the spectre of the slum apocalypse is
not much of a critical alternative to the likes of the UN-Habitat
report *Challenge of the Slums*, which already offers a cultural

framework fearful of the consequences of social exclusion in urban areas and the environmental consequences of urbanisation.[52] Perhaps *Planet of Slums* is better understood as a complementary appendix to the UN-HABITAT report, surfing the territory between the real and imaginary worlds to amplify the already febrile fears of many people about the dangers of the modern world.

The concept of a slum apocalypse has two important consequences. Firstly, it sends a strong message that control over the future is no longer possible. There is little attempt in this imaginative take on the coming catastrophe to offer any explanation for the conditions in emerging cities, and the reader seems likely to conclude that this is a world beyond control. In the event, all that seems to be open to us is to look on uncomprehendingly from the sidelines as events unfold. In fact this is precisely the approach some have taken. Under the heading 'The New African Jungle', one critic argues that 'Africa is historically ill-equipped to build great cities – there are no reference points. The African city is simply happening, a causality without thought, without planning, without ambition.'[53]

Secondly, as this imaginative tale of the slum apocalypse progresses, the urbanising masses become completely dehumanised. Instead of the migrants encountered earlier in this chapter, who come to cities with determined dreams of self-improvement, we are left with people living in such depravity that no action is considered beyond them. In Accra, the Metropolitan Chief Executive is quoted as reporting that '75 per cent of the waste of black polythene bags in the metropolis contains human aborted foetuses'.[54] But instead of stopping to question this fanciful testament to degeneracy, we move breathlessly onwards, past the kidney farms of Madras, the child witches of Kinshasa, to arrive finally at 'an existential ground zero beyond which there are only death camps, famine and Kurtzian horror'.[55] Whatever the intention, this human horror story can serve only to confirm the people of emerging cities as either barbarians or victims; not subjects making their own history, but objects in need of western intervention or sympathy.

SLUM TOURISTS

'It has become fashionable to visit the slum', muses Charity Mupanga, protagonist in *Last Orders at Harrods*, a fictionalised account of life in Nairobi by former *Financial Times* Africa editor Michael Holman.[56] Enthused by what Holman provocatively labels 'well written accounts of squalor and death', films such as *The Constant Gardener*, and the public art of French artist JR, the trail of visitors to inspect the natives of Kibera have ranged from Bill Bryson to sports stars, actors and celebrities including Serena Williams and Drew Barrymore.

Slum tourism is a Nairobi growth industry. Tours organised by the likes of Victoria Safaris (highly recommended on Trip Adviser[57]) include meetings with residents, access to HIV-orphaned children's homes, bio-gas projects, and viewings of the 'innovative' use of animal bones to make ornaments.[58] Slum tourism has been said to have originated with the wealthy New Yorkers who, in the late nineteenth century, snaked along the Bowery and through the Lower East Side to see 'how the other half lives'.[59] Today, stars like Madonna drop into the developing world to save those who cannot be trusted to help themselves.[60]

Within walking distance of Kibera, in a campus of 'bucolic tranquillity'[61] whose well-watered, undulating lawns contrast starkly with the open sewers of the slum, lies the world headquarters of UN-HABITAT.[62] Campaigning for closer relationships between civic society and non-governmental organisations, the organisation provides a focus for the proliferation of non-official groups intervening in how Nairobi develops. Reports of between 6,000 and 15,000 organisations at work in Kibera are surely exaggerated.[63] But even the sober estimate of 700 NGOs tells of the extent to which Kibera has become a 'cause'.[64]

It is difficult not to be reminded of Victorian London, where a charity for every symptom of collective sin and personal pain ensured that the emerging city became honeycombed with missions, brotherhoods and other worthy organisations. But whereas the endeavours of those offering salvation might then have been rooted in evangelical beliefs, today's slum tourists seem to be more motivated by their own absence of any clear moral virtues. At least the zeal of Victorian missionaries – of the Leysian and Wesleyan missions, for example – was directed towards helping people to become educated, well-fed and socially improved. Moralism and Christianity were just some of the mechanisms used, but at least they offered a way up. By contrast, today's missionaries are merely citing the new gospel of health, safety, gender relations and ethical behaviour. The contemporary slum-dweller, it seems, does not need wealth, better homes or a job, but only protection from the dodgy 'booze dens' fuelling crime, violence against women and children, and the modern sins of unsafe sex and over-procreation.[65]

After spending time in the grim workrooms of London, Madox Ford was moved to note the ideals of families living in gruelling circumstances: work; keep off the rates; bring up the kids well; and keep 'them enquiry blokes' (charity organisations) away.[66] Nowadays, among those airing fears that in emerging cities we can see the return of the world described by Dickens, a one-sided focus on squalor undermines a more rounded picture. Yes, Dickens captured the dirt and filth, and told of Tom-all-Alone's. But in Dickens's most personal work, the young David Copperfield saw London as 'an amazing place … fuller of wonders and wickedness than all the cities of the earth'. Emerging cities are more complex and contradictory places than many stories today allow. Certainly, Dickens's portrayal of social conditions was intended to elicit a response; but, as the Oxford academic John Carey points out, behind the corpses and effigies were imaginative ideas. The materials of horror may be there, but they are transmuted, not least by humour, into something more spirited and resilient.[67]

CELEBRATING FLUX

Above all else, the emerging city can be understood as representing the promise of exciting newness and unlimited possibilities.[68] This applies as much to Nairobi, Mumbai and Istanbul today as it did to Paris, London and New York in the nineteenth century. Yes, there may be hellish poverty, slums that almost defy description, conditions that should not be allowed in the twenty-first century. But eco-pragmatists who see in slums a means to save the planet should be treated with contempt, as should those who accept that slums are an inevitable step along the road to a better life. It is not necessary to suffer in order to thrive. To those who blithely excuse slums as a healthy indication that markets are working to pull people up, it should be pointed out that slums actually reflect a lack of dynamism in most economies, and the timidity of risk-averse elites. The existence of slums should be seen as a reflection of a burning need for dynamism and growth.

However, at a time when the emerging city is commonly viewed as an environmental and social disaster, it is worth recognising that there is a bigger picture. What is observable in the slums of Dhaka, Rio de Janeiro, Shenzhen and Tehran is history in the making: this is the latest generation of adventurers keen to make something of themselves and improve their lives.

Suketu Mehta's *Maximum City* describes Bombay as a place of such energy that its inhabitants occupy an imaginative space that appears vastly to exceed the physical boundaries of the city.[69] Theirs are places that resist being defined and confined, but instead open up a space where dreams can be played out – where alongside the poverty, pollution and violence is a pulsating world of opportunities, excitement and experimentation. Such cities are rarely coherent, cohesive entities that operate according to the whim of planners and designers – for which fact we should be thankful. That is not to argue against planning, but merely to recognise that cities sometimes have a dynamism that pushes them beyond expectations.

In eighteenth-century Paris, the phrase 'le tourbillon social'[70] was used to describe the wonder and dread of the whirlwind that new arrivals found themselves thrown into. In the perpetual clash of groups and cabals, a continual flux and re-flux of prejudices and conflicting opinions was a sign that life comes alive once removed from the stultifying comforts of the village. 'Everything is absurd, but nothing is shocking, because everyone is accustomed to everything.'[71] In America, too, many of the downtrodden masses arriving in the new world in the 1800s

50 The Lure of the City

were in for a rough life in the ghettos. The misery and crowding of the immigrant swarm on the Lower East Side was easily the equal of the slums in Bombay today. But each new arrival, invigorated by the 'American dream', knew that things were – potentially – on the up.

In her account of what she calls 'Weimar Istanbul', resident Claire Berlinski compares the city to Berlin, telling of the dread and exhilaration of a city on the verge of political catastrophe, but where a sudden liberalisation has also unleashed the social and political imagination. Her Istanbul today is vast – filled with promise, loneliness, wonderment, poverty, dreams, creativity, art, violence, energy, paranoia, freedom, mysticism, experimentation, anxiety, vice and glamour. Such a city thrives on being in a perpetual state of flux. 'The Old World had vanished', she observes, and gone is 'its agrarian economy, its reassuring class distinctions and social order. An alien and fragile political order had been imposed in its place. Experimental music, art, and cinema flourished; fascinations arose with utopianism, fortune-telling, mysticism, communism.'[72]

Berlinski's celebration of the cultural, social and political life-forces of Istanbul offers a powerful riposte to those who look at emerging cities and see only slums, who interpret life there as little more than the exhausting quest for survival. As Suketu Mehta observes of Bombay, it is possible to see beyond the wreck of a physical city and to revel in the incandescent life-force of its inhabitants.[73] In the west today, where restraint is elevated over free will, observing limits over exceeding the boundaries, ethical behaviour over realising dreams, and playing safe over experimentation, the emerging city provides a suitable reminder of that famous aphorism: *Stadtluft macht frei.*

NOTES

1. Doug Saunders, *Arrival Cities: How the Largest Migration in History is Reshaping Our World*, Heinemann, 2010.

2. UN-HABITAT, *State of the World's Cities 2010/2011 – Cities for All: Bridging the Urban Divide*, 2010, p. 5.
3. Ibid., p. iv.
4. Subir Roy, 'India Will Need New Cities and They Will Require New Powers', *City Mayors Development*, 23 February 2008, at <www.citymayors.com/development/india-new-cities.html>.
5. Parag Khanna, 'Beyond the City Limits', *Foreign Policy*, September–October 2010.
6. UN-HABITAT, *State of the World's Cities 2010/2011 – Cities for All: Bridging the Urban Divide*, Section 1, p. 8.
7. UN-HABITAT, *State of the World's Cities 2008/2009 – Harmonious Cities*, 2010, Section 1, p. 8.
8. UN-HABITAT, *State of the World's African Cities 2010: Governance, Inequality and Urban Land Markets*, 2010, p. viii.
9. James Thomson, *City of the Dreadful Night*, 1874, at <emotionalliteracyeducation.com/classic_books_online/ctdnt10.htm>.
10. UN-HABITAT, *State of the World's Cities 2010/2011 – Cities for All: Bridging the Urban Divide*, Section 1, pp. v, 28.
11. Jerry White, *London in the Nineteenth Century*, Vintage, 2007, p. 477.
12. Ford Madox Ford, *The Soul of London: A Survey of a Modern City*, Everyman, 1995 [1905].
13. Marshal Berman, *All That Is Solid Melts Into Air*, Verso, 1983, p. 345.
14. Madox Ford, *Soul of London*, p. 15.
15. Ibid., p. 13.
16. Ministry of Nairobi Metropolitan Development, *Nairobi Metro 2030: A World Class African Metropolis*, 2008.
17. Mike Davis, *Planet of Slums*, Verso, 2006, p. 138.
18. UN-HABITAT, *State of the World's Cities 2010/2011 – Cities for All: Bridging the Urban Divide*, p. 54.
19. Ibid., pp. 54, 194.
20. Rasna Warah, 'How the Numbers Game Turned Kibera into the Biggest Slum in Africa', *Nation*, 12 September 2010, at <www.nation.co.ke/oped/Opinion/-/440808/1009446/-/view/printVersion/-/u16wcjz/-/index.html>.
21. Robert Neuwirth, *Shadow Cities*, Routledge, 2005.

22. Ibid., pp. 67–99.
23. White, *London in the Nineteenth Century*.
24. Friedrich Engels, *The Condition of the Working Class in England*, Penguin Classics, 2009 [1845], p. 71.
25. Neuwirth, *Shadow Cities*, pp. 67–99.
26. Ibid., p. 16.
27. Ibid., p. 70.
28. Saunders, *Arrival Cities*.
29. Ibid., pp. 63–9.
30. Suketu Mehta, *Maximum City: Bombay Lost and Found*, Headline Review, p. 557.
31. Fay Schlesinger, 'The Slumdog Millionheir: Prince Charles to Build Shanty Town for 15,000 as an Indian Version of Poundbury', *Daily Mail*, 10 January 2011.
32. Ibid.
33. Engels, *Condition of the Working Class in England*, p. 68.
34. Tristram Hunt, 'Introduction', in Friedrich Engels, *Condition of the Working Class in England*, p. 28.
35. Engels, *Condition of the Working Class in England*, p. 68.
36. Daniel Ben-Ami, *Ferraris For All: In Defence of Economic Progress*, Policy Press, 2010, p. 201.
37. David Satterthwaite, 'Barbara Ward and the Origins of Sustainable Development', International Institute for Environment and Development (UK), 2006.
38. Tristram Hunt, *Building Jerusalem: The Rise and Fall of the Victorian City*, Phoenix, 2004, p. 155.
39. 'The Cocoyoc-Declaration', 23 October 1974, at <www.juerg-buergi.ch/Archiv/EntwicklungspolitikA/EntwicklungspolitikA/assets/COCOYOC_%20DECLARATION_1974.pdf>.
40. Martin Ravallion, 'Urban Poverty', *Finance and Development* 44: 3 (September 2007).
41. Professor Tim Jackson, 'Prosperity Without Growth? The Transition to a Sustainable Economy', Sustainable Development Commission, 2009.
42. Stewart Brand, 'Save the Slums', *Wired* 211 (September 2009).
43. Stewart Brand, 'How Slums Can Save the Planet', *Prospect*, 27 January 2010.

44. Massachusetts Institute of Technology, 'What is Slum Upgrading? Overview', at <web.mit.edu/urbanupgrading/upgrading/whatis/what-is.html>.
45. Neuwirth, *Shadow Cities*, p. 236.
46. Schlesinger, 'Slumdog Millionheir'.
47. Neuwirth, *Shadow Cities*, p. 236.
48. Ibid., p. 22.
49. Davis, *Planet of Slums*.
50. Ibid., p. 9.
51. Oswald Spengler quoted in Africa Baobab, 'The New African Jungle', *Economist Online*, 20 October 2010, at <www.economist.com/blogs/baobab/2010/10/africas_cities>.
52. UN-HABITAT, *The Challenge of the Slums – Global Report on Human Settlements*, 2003, p. 124.
53. Africa Baobab, 'New African Jungle'.
54. Davis, *Planet of Slums*, p. 135.
55. Ibid., p. 198.
56. Michael Holman, *Last Orders at Harrods: An African Tale*, Abacus, 2005, p. 19.
57. Trip Advisor, 'Nairobi: Kibera Slum Tour', at <www.tripadvisor.com/Travel-g294207-c148580/Nairobi:Kenya:Kibera.Slum.Tour.html>.
58. African Adventure Company: Victoria Safaris, at <www.victoriasafaris.com/kenyatours/propoor.htm>.
59. Kennedy Odede, 'Slumdog Tourism', *New York Times*, 9 August 2010.
60. Alice Miles, 'Shocked by Slumdog's Poverty Porn', *Times Online*, 14 January 2009.
61. Economist Survey of Cities, 'The Strange Allure of the Slums', *Economist*, 3 May 2007.
62. Neuwirth, *Shadow Cities*, p. 241.
63. Warah, 'How the Numbers Game Turned Kibera into the Biggest Slum in Africa'.
64. Brian Ekdale, 'Playing the Numbers Game to Discredit the Numbers Game', 12 September 2010, available at <www.brianekdale.com/?tag=population>.
65. *Economist*, 'African Moonshine: Kill Me Quick', 29 April 2010.
66. Madox Ford, *Soul of London*, p. 61.

67. John Carey, *The Violent Effigy: A Study of Dickens' Imagination*, Faber & Faber, 1973, pp. 93, 207.
68. Gyan Prakash *Mumbai Fables*, Princeton University Press, 2010.
69. Mehta, *Maximum City*.
70. Berman, *All That Is Solid Melts Into Air*, p. 18.
71. Ibid.
72. Claire Berlinski, 'Weimar Istanbul', *City Journal* 20: 4 (Autumn 2010).
73. Mehta, *Maximum City*, p. 587.

3
The Crowded City
People on the Move

Patrick Hayes

Society does not consist of individuals, but expresses the sum of interrelations, the relations within which these individuals stand … a rich totality of many determinations and relations.

Karl Marx, *Grundrisse*

'In 1819, the British poet Shelley wrote, "Hell is a city much like London." If he were alive today, the poet might have put it differently: "Hell is a city much like Cairo, Calcutta, Shanghai, Bangkok, London, Los Angeles, Mexico City and dozens of others."' So writes Daniel Chiras in *Environmental Science*, one of the standard academic textbooks on the topic, which claims to introduce students to the 'root causes of environmental problems'. In the eyes of Chiras, one 'root cause' stands out above the rest: 'Population is at the root of virtually all environmental problems, including pollution and resource depletion, as well as many social and economic problems.'

The more of us there are, Chiras tells students of environmental science, the greater the problems. And the more we are concentrated in particular spaces, the more the problems multiply:

crowding in urban centres has been implicated in a variety of social, mental and physical diseases. Many social psychologists assert that divorce, mental illness, drug and alcohol abuse, and social unrest result, in part, from stress caused by crowding. Prenatal death and rising crime rates may also be attributed partly to overcrowding. They label this malaise the inner city syndrome.

But not only do crowded cities encourage us, apparently, to become mentally ill, or drug addicts, or to kill unborn babies and breed criminals, they also destroy the environment: 'Cities throughout the world are centres of intense pollution from automobiles, factories, power plants and sewage treatment plants ... as cities spread they expand onto farmland and open space, literally devouring the resources they need to survive and prosper.'[1]

These remarks about crowding in cities are presented to students as a balanced perspective in a textbook that purports to 'take care to show both sides of the debate'. In the West, in much of the current discussion around the nature of cities, they are seen to be symptomatic of an ever-increasing problem – namely, 'too many people'. With only 'finite resources', so the argument goes, as the population heads towards 7 billion, there will be more humans than the Earth can cope with. This is what is often called the 'demographic time-bomb'. The idea that has gained prominence is that there are too many humans around, and that we are killing the planet. Certainly there can be no dispute about two things – more people are living in cities than ever before, and that number is set to increase substantially over the coming decades. As the United Nations' *State of the World's Cities 2010/11* report puts it, 'the world is inexorably becoming urban'.[2]

In 1950, only 28.8 per cent of the world's population was urban; in 2011 the figure stands at just over half of the population. By 2050, the proportion of people on the planet living in urban areas is expected to have risen to 68.7 per cent.[3]

The number of cities is also growing, as is their size. In 1800 London was the largest city, with 1 million people; but by 1960, there were 111 cities with more than 1 million people. According to the UN Population Fund, there are now more than 300. Take also the number of cities containing 10 million inhabitants or more – commonly dubbed 'mega-cities'. In 1950 there was only one (New York), while by 1975 the number had grown to five – and it is expected to reach 26 by 2015.[4]

All developing regions across the planet, including Africa, are expected by the UN to have more people living in urban than rural areas by 2030. As noted in *State of the World's Cities*: 'In the next 20 years, *Homo sapiens*, "the wise human", will become *Homo sapiens urbanus* in virtually all regions of the planet.'[5]

There are good reasons for this growth. People migrate to cities looking for a better life for themselves and their children. Wages are typically higher in cities than in rural areas, and a higher material standard of living can result in longer, healthier lives. Not only do cities offer people the chance to better their lot with higher-skilled and salaried jobs, but there tend to be more creative jobs on offer, and communications are better. The potential to develop a wider network of social relationships, share ideas and live in close proximity to the cultural wealth of society appeals to many. Admittedly this is not always clear-cut. The city is also a place of heartache, and can be filled with squalor and poverty for some; but the overarching progressive dynamic is one of social improvement, even if it is not linear and always obvious.

However, instead of saying 'three cheers' and celebrating this historic movement to cities, the mainstream approach today is to voice concern about the unsustainable growth of cities. Anna Tibaijunka, executive director of UN-HABITAT, the United Nations agency for human settlements, argues, 'as cities sprawl, turning into unmanageable megalopolises, their expanding footprints can be seen from space. These hotbeds of pollution are a major contributor to climate change'.[6] Ronald Wright, in *A Short History of Progress*, concurs: 'A small village on good land beside a river is a good idea; but when the village grows into a city and paves over the good land, it becomes a bad idea.'[7]

Not only are cities said to be destroying the planet, they are also making life more unbearable. Not only is overpopulation seen to be an issue, but the resulting overcrowding is viewed as problematic too. Thomas Friedman succinctly sums up the situation as he sees it in his book *Hot, Flat and Crowded*: '[I]f you think the world feels crowded now, just wait a few decades.'[8]

In his use of the word 'feels', Friedman reveals the sentiment underlying the overcrowding debate. It is a use of 'subjective' language similar to that observed by Frank Furedi in his work

Population and Development, where he noted that in the 1970s the environmentalist Paul Ehrlich also described the 'feel of overpopulation'. As Furedi points out,

> Interpretations based on crude numbers tend to be arbitrary, since in reality human beings cope differentially according to their social arrangements. Terms like overcrowding and overpopulation are value judgements that often masquerade as facts. Over two thousand years ago, wealthy aristocrats were building villas in the countryside surrounding Rome on the grounds that the city was overcrowded. "Overcrowded" cities would not be cities if they had the population densities characteristic of rural areas. Ironically many young people cannot wait to leave their towns of origin for the big overcrowded cities. Others renounce the same urban condition because they consider it inconsistent with healthy living.[9]

To some, then, the city may feel overcrowded, especially while social and economic disparities continue to grow. But this should be understood as a failure of ambitious politics, rather anything inherently wrong with either urbanism or the number of people who live in a place. For some, however, the classic line in Jean-Paul Sartre's *Huis Clos* – 'Hell is other people' – seems apposite. Paul Ehrlich explains his Damascene conversion to restrictive population thinking:

> I came to understand [the population explosion] emotionally one stinking hot night in Delhi a few years ago ... The streets were alive with people. People eating, people washing, people sleeping. People visiting, arguing, and screaming. People ... begging. People defecating and urinating. People clinging to buses. People herding animals. People, people, people, people.[10]

The difficulty in maintaining objectivity in questions of overcrowding means that responses to this increase tend to say more about the underlying values of the individual concerned than about broader society. Like 'congestion', another word that is ill-defined but commonly used to suggest there are too many people, such terms have little to say about the way that, historically, humans have coped. Bickering over definitions of what it feels like to experience overcrowding or congestion may sound like an academic, dinner party preoccupation; but there are serious practical consequences resulting from such discussions. Not the least of these is that such subjective concepts are often used as 'evidence' to support claims regarding overpopulation.

CITIES 'PACKED TO BLACKNESS'

The debate around overcrowding in cities is hardly a new one. As we have already seen, it dates back at least as far as ancient Rome. After all, 2,000 years ago Rome was the first city to reach 1 million people. However, in its present form, the debate would not have been unfamiliar to those living in the West in the nineteenth century. Indeed, perhaps the most renowned theorist of population growth was the Reverend Thomas Malthus, who in his 1798 book *Essays on the Principles of Population* calculated that the rate of population growth would increase exponentially, and thus much faster than it takes to increase the rate of food production: 'The power of population is infinitely greater than the power in the earth to produce subsistence for man.' Malthus warned that a 'premature death' would visit the human race, at a time when there were fewer than 1 billion people on the planet. Food shortages he argued, would bring about widespread starvation, as well as 'epidemics, pestilence and plagues'.[11]

The fact that more people now live in both India and China than the entire population of the world when Malthus was alive shows objectively he has been proved wrong. Innovations in agriculture, industry, medicine and transport have created the possibility of the large increase in the size of the population and the growth of cities. However, when Malthus was alive, cities in the UK were certainly growing at an unprecedented rate: in the early nineteenth century, London became the largest city in the world. What has been aptly called humanity's first 'world city' grew to over 2 million inhabitants in 1850, rising to 5 million by the end of the century and 7 million by 1911, reaching a peak of eight million in 1939.

Peter Ackroyd points out in his biography of the city that, by the nineteenth century, London had become 'the city of fog and darkness'. It was, he said, 'packed to blackness' with people, poverty and pollution:

> By 1870 the sheer quantity of life in the city was overwhelming. Every eight minutes, of every day of every year, someone died in London; every five minutes someone was born. There were forty thousand costermongers and 10,000 'winter tramps'; there were more Irish living in London than in Dublin, and more Catholics than in Rome.[12]

However, Ackroyd cites one writer at the time remarking: 'Who could wonder, that men are drawn into such a vortex, even were the penalty heavier than this?' London had become the wonder of the world – the most dynamic hub of industry and commerce that had ever existed.

Despite this, some reacted fiercely against this 'vortex'. Describing London, Lord Rosebery, ex-Chairman of the London County Council, wrote, 'Sixty years ago a great Englishman, Cobbett, called it a wen. If it was a wen then, what is it now? A tumour, an elephantiasis sucking into its gorged system half the life and the blood and the bone of the rural districts.'[13] And in *To-Morrow: The Peaceful Path to Real Reform*, written in 1898 (and subsequently republished as *Garden Cities of Tomorrow*), Ebenezer Howard deplored that people would 'continue to stream into already over-crowded cities, and … thus further deplete the country districts'.[14] He was fearful of a decline in British agrarian communities.

In a phrase that was to be adapted many years later by Prince Charles when he spoke of a proposed extension to the National Gallery in London as 'a monstrous carbuncle on the face of a much loved and elegant friend', Howard described cities as 'ulcers on the very face of our beautiful island'. In fact, his remarks articulated a significantly different perspective to the those of the conservative prince. Howard was striving to improve the lot of the city-dweller. He saw the terrible conditions of urban centres as a blot on the reputation of civilised advance, saying it should not be the case that 'crowded, ill-ventilated, unplanned, unwieldy, unhealthy cities – ulcers on the very face of our beautiful island – are to stand as barriers to the introduction of towns in which modern scientific methods and the aims of social reformers may have the fullest scope in which to express themselves'.[15]

As London grew in the nineteenth century, rather than attempting to restrict the size of the city, measures were taken to invest in ways to accommodate residents more effectively – albeit often for economic as much as humanist reasons. As Ackroyd notes, as early as 1850, the development of better infrastructure and cheaper fares meant that working-class suburbs began to develop in areas such as Tottenham and East Ham, inducing many people to move out of inner-city regions.[16]

The belief that cities could be improved by the imposition of higher standards was evident from the introduction of building codes, initially as a response to the Great Fire of London of 1666. By the 1870s, as the population increased, so also did ambitions concerning the scale of improvements that could be achieved. As the World Bank has noted, the government 'passed legislation for strict building regulations, prescribing the dimensions of streets and houses, and making it mandatory that all dwellings be connected to newly built sewerage systems. Major municipal investments in water works, sewage facilities, and public health dramatically reduced mortality in Britain's cities between 1874 and 1907.'[17]

The population of cities increased as enclosure of the countryside led to the removal of surplus labour from the fields. But it is worth noting that this division of the land into towns and countryside also led to improvements in agriculture. Rather than 'half the life and the blood and the bone' being sucked out of agricultural districts, technological advances and investment in new machinery led to great improvements in the productivity of agricultural produce – which, in turn, further supported the growth of cities.

Letchworth and Welwyn Garden City represented early attempts to deal with overcrowding, but after the Second World War the influential Abercrombie plans began to disperse crowded neighbourhoods systematically. Around 1.5 million people moved out of London, often into more spacious 'new towns' such as Basildon, Bracknell and Harlow. Others stayed within London, some moving from dense inner neighbourhoods to infill suburbs, and others to new high-rise tower blocks, sometimes built within a landscaped setting.

Consequently, the perceived problems of crowding were dealt with rationally, and, having peaked at 8.6 million in 1939, London's population had dropped to 6.73 million by 1988. While increased immigration rates have boosted the population since then, the current population stands at only around 7.5 million, albeit with a different demographic composition from that of the inter-war years.[18] The twist, however, is that the 'feel' of overpopulation is no longer associated only with dense, crowded centres. Instead, the march of the suburbs into the countryside reinforced the sense that there were too many people, only this time sprawling across the planet. The author of *Sprawl*, Robert Bruegmann, points out the term is 'not so much an objective reality as a cultural concept', which suggests that it is a no less subjective attack on population than is 'overcrowding'.[19]

Contra Malthus, the example of London typifies the way in which innovation tends to find ways of providing sufficient resources and offsetting what he saw to be an inevitable problem of population growth and depleting food stocks. What Malthus had failed to see is that, far from being the only variable to consider, population is only one of many. The one most regularly overlooked – especially in today's society – is mankind's ability to surmount obstacles and manipulate nature in creative ways.

MEGACITY OR MISANTHROPY?

Despite these historical examples contesting the original Malthusian thesis, the standard retort is that the 'spirit' of Malthus is still correct, and that humans have in fact been lucky to be able to survive this long. This would have come as no surprise even to Friedrich Engels in 1844, who recognised that if you go along with the underlying assumptions of Malthusians, then 'if we want to be logical, we have to recognise *that the*

earth was already overpopulated when only one man existed.[20]
In other words, innovation to off-set overcrowding is not
guaranteed to pay off. Indeed, if the population kept growing
at the same rate as during the last century for another 900 years,
physicist J. H. Fremlin predicts that the only way to house the
population would be in 'a continuous 2,000-storey building
covering our entire planet'. He even goes further, calculating that
'at any given time it would take only about 50 years to populate
Venus, Mercury, Mars, the moon and the moons of Jupiter and
Saturn to the same population density as Earth'.[21]

For the neo-Malthusians, the problems of the city are
symptomatic of a greater problem – namely, the fundamental
dangers, in their view, of population growth. This is despite
the fact that population is dropping in developed counties,
and urban areas generally. As environmentalist Stewart Brand
points out, 'On every part of every continent and in every
culture (even Mormon), birth rates are headed down. They
reach replacement level and keep on dropping.'[22] Putting this
situation in perspective further, P. J. O'Rourke calculated that
'at the Manhattan population density of 52,415 per square mile
– everybody on earth can live in former Yugoslavia'.[23]

O'Rourke was writing in 1994, when the population was
about 5.7 billion, so we might need to upgrade his example
somewhat, perhaps to a country the size of North Korea. But
even so, this global Manhattan would still only cover 0.08
per cent of the world's total landmass. The intention behind
thought-experiments such as Fremlin's is to go to the furthest
extreme to accept a key Malthusian tenet – that there are limits
to population growth and, as a result, action needs to be taken.
Experience, and a belief in humanity's ability to overcome
obstacles in future, show that such thought-experiments are
needlessly constrained. Such nightmare scenarios should be
rejected out of hand every time.

However, an underlying Malthusian attitude persists:
modern-day misanthropes may have largely abandoned their
scaremongering over mass starvation, but campaigning in the
name of the planet continues. We are consuming too much,
changing the climate in the process, while draining the planet of

resources. Despite the countless examples of human innovation and ingenuity that have confounded the naysayers over the past two centuries, the sense is that innovations will no longer provide a solution to the *scale* of development now underway. The argument favoured by neo-Malthusians is that developing countries have vastly larger populations than the industrialising countries in the nineteenth century. We could cope back then, with just London and New York expanding; but what about 26 mega-cities? One rumoured proposal in China – a city of 46 million people on a land mass just twice the size of Wales – has been rejected by officials, but it still sparked media paranoia.[24] A World Bank development report shows that 'between 1985 and 2005, the urban population in developing countries grew by more than 8.3 million a year.' That amounts to almost three times the annual increase in population that took place in today's high-income countries between 1880 and 1900 – a time when their incomes were comparable with those of developing countries today.[25]

RISING EAST

While many commentators say they have no problem with cities per se, what they tend to object to is the messy, disorganised way that they develop – but this is to forget the way in which, historically, Western cities emerged. As is noted by Paul James, director of the UN Global Compact Cities Programme, writing in favour of restricting the growth of cities in the *Economist*,

> Living in compact, well-planned, walkable and integrated cities is part of the solution to the issue of global sustainability. The problem is rather the kind of cities that we tend to create: sprawling and bloating. In the global south we see the worst of those excesses, with the burgeoning of hinterland slums, increasing at 6 million people per annum.[26]

Arguably the primary charge made against the growth of cities is the rise of slums on their outskirts, symbolic of their 'sprawling and bloating' nature: as cities rise, millions of people are having to live in cramped and unpleasant conditions. Writing on the rise of slums in the developing world, Mike Davis argues that

> the cities of the future, rather than being made out of glass and steel as envisioned by earlier generations of urbanists, are instead largely constructed out of crude brick, straw, recycled plastic, cement blocks, and scrap wood. Instead of cities of light soaring towards heaven, much of the twenty-first-century urban world squats in squalor, surrounded by pollution, excrement and decay. Indeed the one billion city dwellers who inhabit postmodern slums might well look back with envy at the ruins of the sturdy mud homes of Çatal Höyükin Anatolia, erected at the very dawn of city life nine thousand years ago.[27]

Many see no exit for what economist Paul Collier characterised as the 'bottom billion', living in an 'unlucky minority' of countries 'stuck' at the bottom.[28] Commenting on that urban flow, British environmental campaigner Jonathon Porritt says that it is 'blindingly obvious that completely unsustainable population growth in most of Africa will keep it permanently, hopelessly stuck in deepest, darkest poverty'.[29]

Certainly, the number of slum-dwellers around the world, which the *Economist* estimates at 830 million, is still rising. But the situation may not be as bleak as writers like Porritt make out. While the absolute number of people living in slums is rising, proportionally this figure is in decline: over the past decade the proportion of city-dwellers living in slums has dropped from 40 per cent to less than a third, despite the urban population having grown by over 600 million during that period.

The rise of slums in large cities is a typical feature of rapid urbanisation – as the population rises rapidly, makeshift slums and shantytowns do indeed swell. But the mistake made by those such as Porritt is to see them as a permanent blight on the urban landscape. As urbanist Jane Jacobs has written, 'cities don't lure the middle class. They create it … A metropolitan economy, if it's working well, is constantly transforming many poor people into middle-class people, many illiterates into skilled people, many greenhorns into competent citizens.'[30] The question is that of how to make the metropolitan economy – and its society – work well.

The *Economist* shows that 'China and India have together lifted 125 [million] people out of slum conditions in recent years'. But it is not just the BRIC countries that have made important strides in this area: North Africa's slum population has also shrunk by 20 per cent.[31] There are countless examples of cities that have entirely eradicated their slum populations – from Dublin, Glasgow and Melbourne in the nineteenth century, to Shanghai, Guangzhou and Bogotá in the past couple of decades. The World Bank's report concurs:

> [F]or 'world' cities such as London, New York, Paris, Singapore, and Tokyo, slums can, with the benefit of hindsight, be viewed as part of their 'growing pains.' Britain cleaned up its Dark Satanic Mills over a century ago, and if it had started the cleanup sooner, the working class would have suffered from slower wage growth and lower consumption.[32]

The fact is that, not surprisingly, growing pains are painful. But what would it mean to try to stay the 'growing pains' of rapidly developing urban areas by restricting their population growth? As the authors of the report point out,

> No country has grown to middle income without industrializing and urbanizing. None has grown to high income without vibrant cities. The rush to cities in developing countries seems chaotic, but it is necessary. It seems unprecedented, but it has happened before. It had to have, because the move to density that is manifest in urbanization is closely related to the transformation of an economy from agrarian to industrial to post-industrial.[33]

While it would be naive to celebrate the 'chaos' of the rush to cities in developing countries, to try to slow this development down – to ensure a 'sustainable', managed flow of people to the cities – could end up stunting the growth of such cities, and locking vast numbers into rural poverty. This may sound preferable to some NGOs and fair-trade organisations – what economist Daniel Ben-Ami characterises as 'growth sceptics', namely those who 'see economic growth and popular prosperity as problematic'.[34] However, despite this, most recognise that the tide of people heading towards the cities in developing countries would be impossible to stem.

INDIA: A DEMOGRAPHIC DIVIDEND, OR TIME-BOMB?

Paul Ehrlich's despair, noted above, of the 'people, people, people, people' he saw in Delhi led him to argue that India could not possibly feed all its people – and, notoriously, even to encourage the US to cut off all food aid. Ehrlich underestimated the scope for improvements. There were only 560 million people in India when he was writing in 1971, and now there are almost 1.2 billion; even though, tragically, 350 million or so go hungry, more people are fed and nourished than the entire population of India in Ehrlich's day.

Arguably, nothing characterises the changing nature of India more effectively than Mumbai, currently the densest city in the world, with a population estimated at over 20 million. Some areas of the city apparently manage to accommodate approximately 1 million people within a single square mile – although the figures are hard to verify. The Dharavi slums, made internationally famous by the film *Slumdog Millionaire*, are crammed full of small, ramshackle houses, often homes to dozens of people, lined up in rows that are often separated from one another by impossibly narrow alleyways. These exist alongside small shops, schools, places of worship, small workplaces, and 'hutment' factories making goods from belts to mobile phone covers and kites. Dharavi makes use of every inch of available space. However, as the Hollywood film brought out, and as a visit to Dharavi shows, what is striking about the area is a sense of transition – of people aspiring to improve themselves, to rid themselves of their degrading conditions and better their standards of living.

Increasingly rapidly, Mumbai is beginning to develop ambitious new plans for infrastructural developments, such as the Bandra–Worli Sea Link, a sea bridge 5.6 kilometres in length that cuts the hour's drive from the two areas of the city through heavily congested areas down to a mere seven minutes, which is already transforming movement around Mumbai. There are already ambitious plans to develop this further, including a network of tunnels alongside a Mumbai metro–rail link, a ring railway and truck terminal.

Meanwhile, personal mobility is set to improve substantially with the introduction of affordable cars like the Tata Nano, which are made possible through design innovations and a reduction in the cost of car parts. These developments will inevitably bring about slum clearances and evictions. But it is to be hoped that the long-term improvements to the city will be viewed in the future as having been beneficial to all, including those whose immediate livelihoods were adversely affected.

The UN's *State of the World Cities 2010/2011* report claims that India has managed to lift 59.7 million people out of slum conditions since the year 2000, with the proportion of Indians living in slums falling from 41.5 per cent in 1990 to 28.1 percent in 2010. The report also observes that India has achieved this by 'building the skills of the urban poor in their chosen businesses and by providing them micro-credit and by providing basic services and development within slum settlements; thus improving living conditions'.[35] Aside from the micro-credit scandals, there is obviously a long way to go, and India remains an extremely poor country. But its direction of travel is towards increased prosperity and growth.

While the trajectory towards prosperity is viewed with concern in the West, in the East it is a cause for celebration. Nowhere is this articulated better than by Nandan Nilekani in his work *Imagining India*, where he speaks enthusiastically about the 'demographic dividend' that India can expect, with 270 million young people due to join the job market in the next two decades. As a millionaire, he might be expected to say that, and his enthusiasm for labour-intensive production undermines the real need for industrialised processes. However, rather than seeing the proliferation of people as a cause for alarm, he instead welcomes them with open arms:

> The crowded tumult of our cities is something I experience [every day] as I navigate my way to my Bangalore office through a dense crowd that overflows from the footpaths and onto the road ... Looking around, I think that if people are the engines of India's growth, our economy has only just begun to rev up ... With growth, our human capital has emerged as a vibrant source of workers and consumers not just for India, but also for the global economy.[36]

This palpable optimism, consciously adopted by Nilekani to confront Ehrlich's 1970s comments about the future of India, contrasts equally with the attitudes of many of the naysayers about cities and urbanisation in the West. Nilekani thereby exposes once again the 'subjective' aspect of attitudes to population growth and crowding, which often say more about the commentator's view of humanity's future prospects than anything else.

SLOWING DOWN LONDON

The concerns raised by Western commentators and environmentalists about population growth focus largely on developing nations. But they are more accurately understood as a reflection of the current cultural malaise in the West. Malthusian attitudes and misanthropy are now mainstream. For example, the BBC's prestigious Reith Lecture was delivered in 2007 by influential economist Jeffrey Sachs, who argued: 'Our planet is crowded to an unprecedented degree [and this is] creating unprecedented pressures on human society and on the physical environment.'[37] Respected author Professor John Gray compares humanity to 'slime mould'. James Lovelock says that the world is suffering a 'plague of people.'

Such condescension reflects the emergence of new fears of overcrowding in the West. Take London for example, where immigration has rebooted population growth in recent years, and a return to the 1930s peak of 8 million or more looks like a real possibility. Despite transformation of infrastructure and housing, which is now of a much higher standard than

during the pre-war period, concerns are being expressed once
more that there are too many people. A spokesperson for the
London Housing Federation, for example, has claimed that
'[o]vercrowding is 21st Century London's shame ... London
may be one of the world's most prosperous cities, but it is clear
that not everyone is sharing the benefits.'[38] Yet this so-called
'epidemic' of overcrowding does not seem to motivate ambitious
plans for infrastructure or house-building programmes that
might resolve whatever deficiencies exist. Indeed, in recent
years the idea of building new infrastructure – higher-capacity,
faster roads, for example – has tended to result only in fears of
attracting more people and increasing overcrowding.

Instead, discussion (and proposed solutions) tend to focus
more on the health and emotional consequences of overcrowding.
Movements such as the 'Slow Down London' organisation
campaign to teach people how to cope with overcrowding.
Charities have written about the problems that overcrowding
can cause, from depression and mental illness to asthma, crime
and impaired cognitive development in children.

One notable recent development has been the increasing
popularity of 'downshifting'. Tracey Smith, founder of
'International Downshifting Week', left the city for good in
protest against its stressful pressure and crowding. But framing
overcrowding in terms of health and stress issues appears to
say little about 'overcrowding' itself. Instead, it seems like an
example of the increasing tendency to reframe societal problems
in terms of individual well being.

Finally, it is worth highlighting one of the problematic
practical consequences of the overcrowding debate. In London,
the twentieth-century decline in population was accompanied
by a demographic shift towards smaller households, the result
being that some individuals, couples and small families managed
to increased their living space – for example a couple might have
occupied a two- or three-room flat. Today, however, acceptance
of the idea that the city is overcrowded, with only a certain
number of rooms to go round, has boosted the idea that some
of us live in 'oversized' accommodation, and should in some
circumstances be forced to downsize, so that an appropriately

sized family can move in. Although welfare cuts may force 'oversized' families out of London, the government's pragmatic use of size limits should not be seen as a Chinese-style limit on population. Nevertheless, in Britain the number of large families is declining, and one-child families are increasing. The *Sunday Times* overstated the case when asserting: 'we are slowly producing a nation of only-children'; but the sentiment it expressed was correct when it added that, 'as China dismantles its one child policy, we are busy creating our own'.[39]

The 'we' in question is not the state, but ourselves, as we succumb to an idea that has become increasingly accepted: that we are overcrowded, that the future looks bleak, and that raising the drawbridge on family life might arrest the dangerous tide of 'people, people, people, people'.

THE IRRECONCILABLE CITY

It is telling that, rather than drawing inspiration from Nilekani and his optimism about how India's 'demographic dividend' will ensure that slums are eradicated and yield a more prosperous future for all, environmentalists and other concerned commentators in the West argue instead that we can all learn lessons from the slums.

The most high-profile statement of this position came from Prince Charles, who praised the 'intuitive grammar' of the Dharavi slums:

> I strongly believe that the west has much to learn from societies and places which, while sometimes poorer in material terms are infinitely richer in the ways in which they live and organise themselves as communities ... It may be the case that in a few years' time such communities will be perceived as best equipped to face the challenges that confront us because they have a built-in resilience and genuinely durable ways of living.[40]

Friends of the Earth concurs: 'In the UK we could do worse than looking to the recycling endeavour of slum-dwellers in places like Dharavi for inspiration … There is a lot to learn from the developing world, where a scavenger mentality, grass roots recycling and sheer necessity can lead to imaginative leaps in redeploying waste.'[41] Similarly, the *Observer* comments that 'for a growing number of environmental campaigners Dharavi is becoming the green lung stopping Mumbai choking to death on its own waste', and that '[i]f you have the patience to look closer, you will find here one of the most inspiring economic models in Asia'.[42]

Serious questions must be asked about the mindset of a person who is as 'inspired' by woefully underdeveloped Mumbai slums as by the rapid economic development taking place in Shanghai, Shenzhen or Hong Kong. The inspirational aspects cannot be that the model leads to greater economic growth or material prosperity. To freeze the Dharavi slums as a 'model' to learn from in terms of organisation is to miss what is remarkable about the place – the fact that it is perpetually in transition, containing an ever-new flow of people, with new factories, buildings and business initiatives starting up and constantly changing, as money flows into the area and people move up the ladder and join the ranks of the 'movers-on'. Dharavi is remarkable as a stepping-stone for people to realise their ambitions; but to celebrate it as an end in itself would be to tear the beating heart, the aspirational element, out of it.

Indeed, having recognised that the move towards urbanisation in developing countries is inevitable, with the failure of almost all policy that has attempted to slow down urbanisation, many commentators are now recognising the need for a change of tack – indeed, recognising that cities can be 'good' for the environment. In so doing, they often further rehabilitate Malthusianism. As the self-styled 'rational optimist' Matt Ridley has put it, we can 'cram people into cities and save the Earth', with buildings such as the Burj Khalifa in Dubai being a 'good thing', since 'the more intensely human beings use the space they take up, the more space they can hand back to Mother Nature'. Architect Ken Yeang believes that the best thing we can do for the planet is to build more skyscrapers, thus minimizing our so-called harmful footprint. In their formulation, human 'impact' is seen as inherently negative and in need of restraint. This is a real problem.

This approach is also enthusiastically adopted by Parag Khanna, director of the Global Governance Initiative:

> In fact, it is urban centres – without which suburbs would have nothing to be 'sub' to – where our leading experiments are taking place in zero-emissions public transport and buildings, and where the co-location of resources and ideas creates countless important and positive spillover effects. Perhaps most importantly, cities are a major population control mechanism: families living in cities have far fewer children.[43]

The UN has also adopted such an approach, arguing that 'paradoxically' cities 'hold our best chance' for a sustainable future: 'The battle for a sustainable environmental future is being waged primarily in the world's cities. Right now, cities draw together many of Earth's major environmental problems: population growth, pollution, resource degradation and waste generation.'[44]

Using this rhetoric, it seems that Malthusians have learned to stop worrying, and increasingly to love cities – but not as productive, exciting, dynamic places; rather, simply because they are a tried and tested way of keeping the population down and reducing our footprint on the Earth. The problem with these arguments, however, is that cities effectively lose their progressive essence of growth and dynamism. In fact, they promote cuts to our consumption and advocate fewer of 'us'. This is not the same as an efficient city; it is merely a misanthropic one. People should be coming to the city for freedom, to transform and develop their lot and realise their aspirations, to transform nature and social barriers – not to be regulated, monitored, downsized and made more efficient, or told we need to operate within the limits of environmental parameters.

As the self-dubbed 'eco-pragmatist' Stewart Brand puts it, 'environmentalists have yet to seize the enormous opportunity offered by urbanisation'. We need, in his view, to '[g]reen the hell out of the growing cities'.[45] However, when cities are seen from a pragmatic, instrumental point of view, driven by misanthropy and with greater consideration given to nature than to the aspirations of humanity, this ideal is less that of a city and more that of a giant battery-farm: cities become arenas that force us to reduce our polluting impact on the planet. In fact, cities are about stamping our impact on the planet. The portrayal of human beings as inherently harmful is a remnant of explicit Malthusianism, and one that is arguably worse – and certainly more insidious – than that of previous generations. Fundamentally, for a civilised society, there is an irreconcilability between Malthusianism and the city.

NOTES

1. Daniel D. Chiras, *Environmental Science*, 8th edn, Jones & Bartlett, 2010, p. 137.
2. UN-HABITAT, *State of the World's Cities 2010/2011 – Cities for All: Bridging the Urban Divide*, 2010, p. x.
3. United Nations Population Information Network, at <www.un.org/popin/data.html>.
4. UN-HABITAT, *State of the World's Cities 2010/2011 – Cities for All: Bridging the Urban Divide*, p. x.
5. Ibid.
6. Linda Starke, *State of the World 2007: Our Urban Future*, Earthscan, 2007, p. xvii.
7. Ronald Wright, *A Short History of Progress*, Carroll & Graf, p. 108.
8. Thomas L. Friedman, *Hot, Flat and Crowded: Why We Need a Green Revolution and How It Can Renew America*, Farrar, Straus & Giroux, 2008, p. 28.
9. Frank Furedi, *Population and Development: A Critical Introduction*, Polity, 1997, pp. 40–1.
10. Paul R. Ehrlich, *The Population Bomb*, Bucaneer Books, 1971, p. 2.
11. Thomas Malthus, *An Essay on the Principle of Population*, Oxford University Press, 1993, p. 61.
12. Peter Ackroyd, *London: The Biography*, Vintage, 2001, p. 594.

13. Ebenezer Howard, *To-Morrow: The Peaceful Path to Real Reform*, Swan Sonnenschein, 1898, p. 3; taken from P. Hall, D. Hardy, E. Howard and C. Ward, *To-Morrow: A Peaceful Path to Real Reform*, Routledge, 2003, p. 21.

14. Howard, *To-Morrow*, p. 3; taken from Hall et al., *To-Morrow*, p. 21.

15. Ebenezer Howard, *Garden Cities of To-Morrow*, Faber & Faber, 1946 [1902], p. 147.

16. Ackroyd, *London*, p. 756.

17. World Bank, *World Development Report 2009: Reshaping Economic Geography*, World Bank, 2009, p. 68.

18. 'GLA Demography Update, October 2008', at <legacy.london.gov.uk/gla/publications/factsandfigures/dmag-update-16-2008.rtf>.

19. Robert Bruegmann, *Sprawl: A Compact History*, University of Chicago Press, 2005, p. 3.

20. Ronald Meek, ed., *Marx and Engels on Malthus*, Lawrence & Wishart, 1953, p. 59.

21. Paul R. Ehrlich, *The Population Bomb*, Buccaneer Books, 1971, p. 5.

22. Matt Ridley, 'Cram People into Cities and Save the Earth', *Sunday Times*, 17 January 2010, at <www.timesonline.co.uk/tol/comment/columnists/guest_contributors/article6990948.ece>.

23. P. J. O'Rourke, *All the Trouble in the World: The Lighter Side of Overpopulation, Famine, Ecological Disaster, Ethnic Hatred, Plague, and Poverty*, Atlantic Monthly Press, 1994, p. 60.

24. Chris Devonshire-Ellis, 'China's Mega City? Er… Hang on a Second', *China Briefing*, 27 January 2011.

25. World Bank, *World Development Report 2009*, p. 12.

26. Paul James, 'The Proposer's Opening Remarks', *Economist*, 11 January 2011, at <www.economist.com/debate/days/view/639/print>.

27. Mike Davis, *Planet of Slums*, Verso, 2006, p. 19.

28. Paul Collier, *The Bottom Billion*, Oxford, 2004, p. 5.

29. Jonathon Porritt, 'If I Was in Government… Jonathon Porritt Makes Population His Number One Issue', *Ecologist*, April 2007.

30. World Bank, *World Development Report 2009*, p. 49.

31. 'Slumdog Millions' *Economist*, 24 March 2010, at <www.economist.com/node/15766578>.

32. World Bank, *World Development Report 2009*, p. 68.
33. Ibid., p. 24
34. Daniel Ben-Ami, *Ferarris for All*, Policy Press, 2010, p. 11.
35. UN-HABITAT, *State of the World's Cities 2010/2011*, p. 39.
36. Nildan Nilekani, *Imagining India: Ideas for the New Century*, Penguin, 2010, p. 35.
37. Jeffery Sachs, 'Bursting at the Seams', Reith Lectures 2007, at <www.bbc.co.uk/radio4/reith2007/lecture1.shtml>.
38. BBC News, '"Overcrowding epidemic" in London', 21 November 2006, at <news.bbc.co.uk/1/hi/england/london/6167560.stm>.
39. Margarette Driscoll, 'O Brother Where Art Thou?' *Sunday Times Magazine*, 20 March 2011.
40. Robert Booth, 'Charles Declares Mumbai Shanty Town Model for the World', *Guardian*, 6 Friday February 2009, at <www.guardian.co.uk/artanddesign/2009/feb/06/prince-charles-slum-comments>.
41. Dan McDougall, 'Waste Not, Want Not in the £700m Slum', *Observer*, 4 March 2007, at <www.guardian.co.uk/environment/2007/mar/04/india.recycling>.
42. Ibid.
43. Parag Khanna, 'When Cities Rule the World', *McKinsey & Company: What Matters*, 7 January 7 2011, at <whatmatters.mckinseydigital.com/cities/when-cities-rule-the-world>.
44. UNFPA, *State of the World Population 2007*, at <www.unfpa.org/swp/2007/english/introduction.html>.
45. Stewart Brand, *Whole Earth Discipline*, Atlantic, 2010, p. 69.

4
The Planned City
Make No Little Plans

Michael Owens

Founding a city in the wilderness is a deliberate act of conquest, a gesture after the manner of the pioneering colonial tradition, and the competitor's conception of such a city would be most important. This is particularly so because the city will not be a result of regional planning but the cause of it: its foundation will lead, later, to the planned development of the whole region.

Lucio Costa, *Report of the Pilot Plan of Brasília*, 1957

The great American urbanist Daniel Burnham, the man who drafted the first comprehensive city plan a century ago, summed up the necessary ambition involved in the art of city-making: 'Make no little plans', he said. 'They have no magic to stir men's blood.'[1]

Such a confident defence of the place of comprehensiveness and scale when applied to the process of building cities and regions has no place in the planning imagination today. Rather, there is a penchant for celebrating the unplanned, open-ended, organic character of cities, exemplified by Richard Sennett's description of Jane Jacobs's view of urban life: 'She believes that in an open city, as in the natural world, social and visual forms mutate through chance variation; people can best absorb, participate, and adapt to change if it happens step-by-lived-step.'[2]

Some with an interest in simplifying the process for approving development advocate city czars and city mayors as a means to bring authority and control to proceedings. The singular figure of the czar might remind some of us of Baron Haussmann's Paris or Robert Moses's New York. On the other hand, many now view such powerful figures with suspicion, and instead promote community involvement in shaping cities and advocate collaborative planning. In this view of planning, the power broker is replaced with the ideal of building good communication and consensus to synthesise multiple opinions and interests. On one side (and looking defeated) stands the model of large-scale change; on the other, incremental and organic development.

In an earlier work, the academic Alan Hudson proposed a planning system in which people determine the future: 'Planners should be told what to do by people, and this would be planning.'[3] He distinguishes between the technical activity of city management through planning, architecture and design, and the act of city development understood as the product of social interaction and social contestation. Hudson situates the failure of the bureaucratic activity of planning within a wider account of the distance between the elite and the people, and in circumstances of economic decline and social fragmentation. So if planning as it exists today is part of the problem and not the solution, how would planning in the service of people be any different? Can people be the subject of planning – its makers, rather than its object?

Or alternatively, is the removal of constraints the best approach? Is it not the case that organic, unfettered urban growth gives rise to a participatory and human self-creation of urban form? As Colin Ward's work on cotters and squatters in Britain[4] showed, 'self-help housing provision is flexible, cheap and creative. It tends to use human capital rather than financial capital, and to evolve slowly from the most basic provision by devising ingenious new solutions.'[5] As the localism agenda gains ground, have we given up on the idea of large-scale urban change?

THE PUBLIC SPHERE

Lewis Mumford's *The City in History* provides an extensive account of the creation of the fabric of cities across history, as rulers took advantage of the concentration of humanity to create order around religion, knowledge and work.[6]

Beginning as a concentration of manpower under a firm, unified, self-reliant leadership, the ancestral city was primarily an instrument for regimenting men and mastering nature, directing the community itself to the service of the gods.[7]

Examples of city development from ancient times onwards show how, in an earlier age, city planning was made possible by the exercise of power and control, and through the development of society's technical capacity to overcome natural limitations like the availability of water and food. Urban patterns have reflected a series of stages: a response to nature; the development of streets and walls; the parcelling out of plots around a core building in medieval cities; and then the imposition of order through zoning. A number of basic urban forms – the grid street system, or star-shaped radial routes emanating from the central core – are consistently repeated.

History offers many fine examples of planned cities: Venice, with its squares and transport routes; Barcelona's dense urban fabric; the iconic buildings and parks of Paris, made visible and linked by wide boulevards. Some basic structural features, including streets, squares and courtyards, endured for centuries in pre-industrial cities The street patterns and public squares of Greek and Roman cities continued to feature in late medieval, Renaissance and baroque city design.[8]

It is not necessarily useful, however, to look to history to provide lessons about how to plan successfully. Streets and public squares might have endured, but they often functioned in radically different ways in response to changing circumstances. Consequently, our perception of successful city forms is often based on a view about the contemporary appropriation of old buildings and places, rather than on their functional success in the period when they were built. The extent to which plans meet society's requirements must be judged in relation to specific historical and social circumstances – not least because the very concept of the public is also historically specific.

Jürgen Habermas explains how the public sphere first appeared in seventeenth-century England, and then developed to assume its character in relationship to the development of the modern state.[9] Civil society emerged in the mercantilist period: a feature of a new kind of state in which power is depersonalised. With the development of a commodity market, economic activity was privatised: labour and capital were traded and invested as the property of private individuals.

In parallel with these developments, the exchange of commodities in supervised market conditions became a public activity: 'the private sphere of society that has become publicly relevant', as Hannah Arendt put it.[10] This forms the context for the development of the modern public sphere. Public discussion, involving private individuals in the town – as distinct from the court of the nobility – developed in the late seventeenth and early eighteenth centuries in the French salons and English coffee houses, and in the pages of the press. These were the historical precursors of the development of the modern state, in which political institutions seek legitimation in public opinion. If the existence of a politically informed public is a modern condition, then few clues are likely to be found in pre-modern societies about how to build a good relationship between people and planning.

URBAN REVOLUTIONS

The age of urban revolution – the century to 1945 – created the modern city. The move of populations from countryside to city continued, voluntarily or as a result of coercion, and then the city reappropriated the countryside through urban and suburban expansion. In common with all of Europe's major cities, the metropoles of Paris and London and New York expanded out of recognition, growing fivefold in size in the nineteenth century.

In the early years of the urban revolution, much urban growth could still legitimately be labelled 'unplanned'. Workers' housing was developed without basic infrastructure such as sewerage and drainage, and outbreaks of cholera and tuberculosis ensued. However, considering simply the history of city-building during the period, it is easy to underestimate the profound social transformation that was taking place. Cities can be characterised not only in terms of the acceleration in the scale and pace of their development, but also in terms of the creation of a different social order. Although much of the fabric created in previous centuries stood still, new property relations and social classes were formed.

We need to situate our understanding of the nature and social function of planning in this historical context. The planning theorist Gordon Cherry makes an important distinction between the act of town-building according to design principles, and town planning in the sense that we now understand it – namely, as an 'extension of public control over private interests in land and property'.[11] Town planning, an aspect of the institutional fabric of the modern state, should not be confused with city building more generally.

In arguably the first comprehensive plan for a modern city, Baron Haussmann, prefect of the Seine, was appointed by Louis Napoleon in 1853 to draw up plans for Paris. He responded with what remains to this day one of the most ambitious plans for a city. Haussmann was very much a product of his era, epitomising the pioneering spirit of the Victorian city-builders in his plans to reshape Paris's street network and transform the city through the creation of ambitious parks, canals and city monuments, as well as a sewerage system.

How do Haussmann's plans for a Modern Paris fare when assessed with reference to the dominant ideas of contemporary planners? In some ways Haussmann's radical solutions disguised the level of their continuity with the old methods of planning: the authoritarian intervention of society's elite, using its power in unambiguous and an unapologetic pursuit of its interests. Famously, the plans for Paris were partly a response to the emergence of an urban working class and the threat that it posed to the social order. Clearly, therefore, his plans were geared towards establishing state control rather than securing the interests of the people.

However, it is important to recognise another side to this story. The new wide streets certainly created easy access for the militia into areas of urban unrest; more importantly, though, they asserted the primacy of movement for commerce, industry and the people – the new urban citizens of Paris.[12] The public may not have been consulted, but the light, air and streetscapes that defined the new city are indelibly associated with the birth of a progressive, modern, urban culture. In addition – unlike today, when the local is celebrated by policy-makers and planners alike – the new streets that were imposed, and which connected up the different areas of the city, in fact met with the progressive aspirations of workers for access across the entire city. No longer were citizens to be confined to their own neighbourhoods.

There are probably few today who would resent the existence of the boulevards that were cut through the dense, medieval tapestry of streets that existed before. Yet would we have the confidence to carry out such changes today? Recent community planning exercises in English cities such as Manchester and Liverpool, conducted in areas of decaying Victorian houses, have progressed on the basis that comprehensive redevelopment must be prevented. Small-scale, selective demolition is now the favoured option. While the communities living in these neighbourhoods have been consulted and engaged, are they better off? And, given that such exercises often progress under the influence of unelected (although supposedly community-friendly) representatives,[13] have communities in fact had any more control over shaping their future? To return briefly to Gordon Cherry's distinction, have people been involved in town-building? Or in town planning?

Two planning currents were to emerge later in the urban revolution that could properly be labelled modern: the Garden City movement, and Modernism itself. Each was predicated on a commitment to comprehensiveness, on the imposition of order based on the application of reason, and on a belief that the future would be a radical improvement on the past – not just for the elite but for the whole of society. Planning too reflected the belief that society could be changed for the better.

Ebenezer Howard, a leading British philanthropist and reformer, and founder of the Garden City movement, was concerned to find solutions to the agrarian, housing and health crises of late-nineteenth-century Britain. In 1898, when he published *To-Morrow: A Peaceful Path to Real Reform*[14] (later reissued as *Garden Cities of Tomorrow*), he advocated the development of small towns of 30,000 people as satellites to British cities. A sense of his ambitions can be gleaned from a statement of intent he delivered to a national town planning conference in 1909:

> We must uprear – no less an aim is worthy of our powers – the most beautiful and harmonious City the world has yet seen – a City of Industry and Commerce, indeed, but also a City of Homes for the people, without one slum or festering sore in all its wide expanse.[15]

Although Howard's schemes were only realised in full at Letchworth and Welwyn, his ideas and values were influential in the Garden Suburb extensions and post-war New Town developments. Developments such as the Lansbury Estate in east London were modern in their comprehensiveness, which sought to tackle a gamut of urban problems such as ill health, poverty, slums and disorder. Whereas Howard developed detailed plans for funding his towns, by the post-war period large-scale schemes were made possible through state planning and the state's control of land and development.

There are a number of striking similarities between post-war plans and those promoted over the past decade. At Lansbury, for example, where proposals embodied the planning vision espoused in the famous County of London plan of 1943,[16] we find a series of neighbourhoods, of between 6,000 and 10,000 people, that would not be out of kilter with the plans of the Urban Task Force–led urban renaissance of today. School, shopping centre and local services also feature, each within walking distance for those living in the neighbourhood.

The substantial difference between then and now, it might be argued, can probably be located in the ability to deliver on such plans. Whereas today multi-partnership but bit-part delivery programmes mean that planners struggle to meet the aspirations of communities, in the post-war period investment and a comprehensive vision for London's reconstruction and growth, overseen by dedicated London County Council planners, made success more likely. And although imposed from above, plans were often well received by a public that was optimistic about the future and keen to consign depression and war to history.

The East End of London had welcomed the Queen during the Blitz; now it welcomed the planners of post-war reconstruction.

The Garden City movement developed concurrently with the emergence of the profession of town planning within the UK, Europe and the USA.[17] And as the Garden City movement ran out of steam, the Modernists – with whom it shared close links within the emerging profession – became an increasingly dominant force, as planning became established within the post-war state apparatus.

BREAK WITH THE PAST

Modernism, in contrast to the agrarian influences within the Garden City movement, was unashamedly urban, promoting an absolute break with the past. Advocating the creation of a new environment for a new society, planning ambitions became closely linked with twentieth-century national visions of progress – encouraging, for example, plans for the communist cities of the Soviet Union; for the new cities of post-colonial countries seeking to make a leap from the conditions of the Third World; for the modernising ambitions of already successful cities such as New York; and, in the UK, for the reconstruction projects of the post-war welfare state.

Planning in this era often engaged in visionary thinking – the production of bold plans intended to fire the imagination on the question of how society might move beyond existing conditions. Planning was intended to create new forms of living, working and interacting, and drew inspiration from the experiments in city planning and architecture in Soviet society in the 1920s, where the Association of Contemporary Architects (OSA) created housing blocks within neighbourhoods to include communal canteens and social clubs, supporting new socialist forms of living. Out went streets bordered by houses (single houses being judged necessary only for large families); in came apartment houses, and hotel-type arrangements supporting public services including laundries and social clubs. In short, the planning of

housing, industry, traffic and public spaces reflected the ambition
to transform social life itself.

Given that planners were often ensconced within state
organisations, we should recall the egalitarian values that
informed the movement more broadly, and its close links to
Soviet planning of the 1920s and the avant-garde Congres
Internationaux d'Architecture Moderne (CIAM).[18] It should also
be recognised, however, that Modernism could sustain an eclectic
political base because its fundamental premise was technical
rather than political: its belief was that urban designs could
usher in social transformation, a proposition that was deployed
to a variety of political ends. However – as art historian Rhodri
Windsor Liscombe records – there was a widespread belief in
the 'efficacy of theoretical modelling in societal re-formation'.
He notes, for example, the bishop of Birmingham's prayer of
1941, in the depths of world war: 'That thou wilt guide all those
who plan the rebuilding of our cities, so that from this midst of
destruction there may rise cities more fair to become the dwelling
place of thy children.'[19]

As is pointed out elsewhere in this book, the city is a place
of conflicts and contradictions. Comprehensive planning also
embodied many contradictions: a belief in egalitarianism was
combined with ambitions of social engineering; radical social
change was pursued together with social stability; a desire for
experimentation coexisted with the incorporation of planning
into the state. Comprehensive planning needs to be considered
in this context of these tensions and contradictions.

One of the most complete realisations of Modernist plans, and
of the manifestos of CIAM, is Brasília, located on the central
plateau of Brazil. Brasília, like Chandigarh in India, was the
product of the modernising ambitions of new states embracing
notions of progress and optimism. Utopian ambitions for the
creation of a new society inspired a radical re-conception of
city life. Plans were promoted by highly centralised government
bodies, backed by massive state intervention, and steered by
expert architects and master planners – in the case of Brasília,
Lucio Costa and Oscar Niemeyer.

In Brasília, many of the main buildings constructed as part of this social experiment were designed by the architect Oscar Niemeyer. To give an indication of the atmosphere that surrounded this utopian project, Niemeyer – a friend of then-President Juscelino Kubitschek – spent the three-year period when the city was being laid out living in the camp with the construction workers.

After the city was completed, James Holston describes how, despite the creation of uniform housing types to serve all sections of society, a rapport between social classes was less in evidence, as the elite moved out to private districts where they socialised in exclusive clubs.[20] If the social engineering of an 'appropriate' mix of people was the aim, then clearly it had failed. But is that what planners should be attempting? And is its failure enough to discredit the experiment? After all, since 1987 the city, as built to the plan of Lucio Costa, has been protected under a UNESCO heritage order.

According to the Edinburgh academic Richard Williams, who has studied the modern architecture of Brazil, the city remains to this day a striking experiment.[21] In moving away from the dominant urban model that values people, traffic, and the flow of goods and services, the comprehensive plan provides an alternative urbanism in which city and landscape are imagined as part of the same system. According to Williams, at least by the middle classes, the sense of inner-urban, wide-open space is greatly appreciated.

But more critical accounts lambast the utopian blueprints of the government and their master planners for an attempt to create a future that radically departs from the past, but fails to generate a city to which rights are equally available to all sections of society. It has been noted that informal settlements have appeared within Brasília, and satellite areas of the city have had the effect of reproducing inequality in housing and employment conditions. Public space has to some extent been privatised through the eradication of the street and the zoning systems. Meanwhile, public access to amenities is often dependent on wealth: many connections presuppose car access, which is limited to the wealthy.

Clearly, none of these developments are desirable, and I return below to the problematic separation of the stated ideals of government and its experts from the real social circumstances of the population. But it is worth noting here that, while the utopian faith in the transformative potential of city planning alone is misguided, the main social problems in Brasília are the product of enduring poverty and inequality, rather than of the built form of the city.

In fact, one of the most interesting lessons of Brasília (and Chandigarh too), is the manner in which people adapt to and exploit that built form. As travel writer Cees Nooteboom notes, people have simply taken possession of both cities.[22] In Brasília, the grounds of some of the monumental architectural masterpieces at weekends become host to bustling informal markets and stalls, bars and barbeques. Shopkeepers use the rear of their premises rather than the front, creating new focal points for public interaction which overcome the eradication of the traditional street. In Chandigarh, while concrete architectural forms have not transformed daily life, neither have they arrested the main cultural expressions of the communities they serve.

City life, it would seem, is unpredictable, constantly subverting expectations. Consequently, some of the best laid plans can give rise to empty people-less zones, while some unpromising urban spaces can become the lifeblood of the city. Large-scale experiments, such as in Brasília, provide the means to look at alternative models of the city. But in the past half-century or so, such bold planning has fallen out of favour.

MODERNISM'S DISCONTENTS

The collapse of the Ronan Point housing block in Newham, east London, in 1968 fuelled the growing perception that the confidence in Modernist towers as the solution to the housing crisis in Britain's cities was deeply ill-founded. The Pruitt–Igoe Projects in St Louis played the same role in America, famously prompting architectural critic Charles Jencks to declare the time of their demolition – 3:32 p.m. on 15 July 1972 – to represent the death of Modernism.

The shocks running right through society were often experienced as a problem of the city itself, particularly within inner-city neighbourhoods. With 'cycle of deprivation' theories blaming the enduring poverty in rundown neighbourhoods on intrinsic, local social factors, an interest both in the politics of neighbourhoods and in community action was born on both sides of the Atlantic. A new focus, language and politics of planning were being forged.

However, urban studies Professor Leonie Sandercock correctly situates the end of Modernism within the context of a wider loss of credulity, writing: 'Modernism has received a bad rap since the 1960s, since Herbert Marcuse, Michel Foucault, and many others put the boot in.'

So the rejection of Modernism cannot be attributed merely to poorly designed estates or dissatisfaction with the processes of planning; rather, it emerged as a reflection of broader societal changes that were occurring in the 1960s. While the focus on Civil Rights movements lends that decade a radical air, culturally the decade can be associated with rejection of universalism in favour of difference, diversity and the local. It is suggested elsewhere in this book that the notion of the metropolitan found expression in the embrace of the idea of moving beyond the parochial. By the 1960s however, the defence of community, which previously might have been held up as a conservative idea, came instead to be identified with radicals.

The most important arena in which the transition from bold ideas to the embrace of community planning was played out was New York in the 1960s. As we have seen, in the post-war period, comprehensive planning became associated as a route out of depression. Modernism's rationalism – the 'manifesto of the straight line'[23] – had found its realisation in the New York skyline, and elsewhere in the USA and Europe. As in the UK, Modernist-inspired social housing developments and comprehensive infrastructural redevelopment became integral parts of that reconstruction project. Robert Moses, the powerful

New York City executive who led a refashioning of the city, played just as much of a part in re-creating the relationship between the city's communications systems and urban space as had Haussmann in reconfiguring Paris. This time, however, the intervention integrated the suburban hinterland with the existing city to transform New York into a new urban region, which today has become the largest urban land area in the world.[24]

By the 1960s, however, such ambitious metropolitan planning ideas were running into significant opposition in some of the local neighbourhoods of New York that were being dismembered by Moses's new highways. Having suggested that 'sometimes you have to hack your way through the city with a meat axe',[25] Moses was portrayed by his critics, often led by journalist and campaigner Jane Jacobs, as a demon who used his power and influence to orchestrate the large-scale displacement of communities to make way for development. As he said, the idea of the megalomaniac prepared to pursue development no matter what the human cost became a motif for opponents of Modernism. For his critics, Moses personified its evils: an aloof assertion of principles imposed from the drawing board, based on abstract principles with no reference to real lives.

Standing in the opposing corner was Jacobs, who in the opening line of her seminal work *The Death and Life of Great American Cities* boldly stated her position: 'This book is an attack on current city planning and rebuilding'.[26] Jacobs had both the Garden City movement and Modernists in her sights. She disliked both suburbs and urban superblocks, seeing in each a 'desire to flee the city': in one case she criticised 'anti-urban' suburban forms and the relocation of development to the countryside; in the other she decried the imposition of zoning and extraneous plans that undermined the informal arrangements and organisation of city life. In the time since the book was published, it has taken on almost biblical status among designers and urban planners, who admire Jacobs's defence of complex, pedestrian-friendly neighbourhoods, against which she counterposes the 'marvels of dullness created by planners'.

COMPLEX CITIES

A number of themes that set the future course of city planning were introduced by Jacobs. Firstly, she positively embraces the notion of the complexity of social life, seeing its informality as a source of the vitality, dynamism and interest that are essential to successful places. For Jacobs, Modernism represented an idealist attempt to impose order and simplicity that had the effect of undermining the ability of a city to generate and respond to complexity.

In the final chapter of *The Death and Life of Great American Cities* she promotes 'organised complexity' and attacks oversimplified planning methods that use too few variables and compartmentalise cities in order to overcome the perceived disorganisation of existing cities – manoeuvres of both the Garden City planners and the Modernists. Jacobs proposes that cities be treated as organisms, implying that they need to be understood by inductive reasoning and by attention to detailed clues, rather than through analysis of the city as a whole. Whereas the Modernists had based their ideas in scientific rationalism, Jacobs found inspiration in the then relatively new science of complexity – whose materialisation has been identified by critics as part of a broader retreat from reason and collapse of belief in the idea that humanity should counterpose itself to nature.[27] Taking inspiration from the life sciences, Jacobs argued that cities should be understood as natural organisms, downplaying the fact that human settlements are created – and planned – as a reflection of social needs and human aspirations. Her view of the city as a problem of organised complexity, growing organically and benefiting most from small-scale interventions, helped provide an intellectual framework for a retreat from the idea of comprehensive planning as a means of pursuing human interests.

The charge that society has become too complex to plan at a large scale does not stick. Global flows of capital have certainly changed the context of planning, though actually the world was economically globalised some centuries ago. The increased speed of communication today, as well as new forms of communication, also create new tools for the formation of communities of interest. We have never been in a better position to make sense of complexity. A trivial example demonstrates the point: the Friendship Wheel, a software application on Facebook, will lay bare in an instant the interconnections in one's social circle. Such revelations, once only fathomable through serious, obsessive research, have become mundane. For planners, Google Earth's Street View augments a visit to a location. Computer-aided design tools simplify city design. Open-source software introduces crowd-sourcing techniques to the planner's armoury. Complexity is reducible. Technological and social change create both new problems and new opportunities on all sides.

Jacobs's proposition that the city is an organism might have some appeal because it acknowledges, no matter what plans are made, that people constantly shape and reshape cities in the course of simply living their lives. It is difficult not to agree with her assertion as to the benefits of free, fluid and intense urban environments that resist a controlling hand. This, after all, is surely what urban life is about?

Yet we might also note the extent to which planning today embraces these notions. It could be argued that those espousing ideas of sustainable communities and new urbanism today are among the foremost admirers of Jacobs and her conception of the city's organic forms. And yet, consider the ambitions that govern their urban designs today – where terms such as 'localism', 'limits', 'safety', 'health' and 'respect' appear regularly. Are these urban or metropolitan ideals, or are they more parochial? Is it now the organic planners who, in Jacobs's words, 'desire to flee the city'? The organic city is contradictory in the sense that it rejects the imposition of controls over nature in the interests of humanity, while endorsing controls over human freedoms in the urban sphere.

COLLABORATIVE PLANNERS

The second important trend associated with the 1960s, and which Jacobs epitomised, is the idea that planning should be a collaborative process. Jacobs attacks the notion of comprehensive change and totalising discourse ostensibly from the left, siding with the people against the authorities. As 1960s radicalism gripped planners along with all of the social professions, it became increasingly unpopular to plan 'for' people; rather, a radical sentiment gained ground whereby planners would seek to side with the poor, the oppressed and the marginalised.

It is now 50 years since Jane Jacobs wrote *The Death and Life of American Cities*. During that same period, a set of planning practices loosely labelled 'collaborative planning' – 'an inclusive dialogic approach to shaping social space'[28] – have become increasingly popular, often badged with the vague epithet 'bottom-up'. The UK government argues that

> citizens should be actively involved in making the kind of decisions hitherto reserved for bureaucrats and elected representatives ... The production of new local plans is a process that is ideally suited to the use of collaborative democracy. By building local plans from the bottom up so that they genuinely reflect the will of the people, we will help communities to come together so they can solve their collective problems together.[29]

The notion that real actions by real people are more important than bureaucratic policies is attractive. Jacobs draws the conclusion that intervention in the city is possible, just as a doctor may address problems in a living organism. Despite her polemic against the Modernist land-use planning of the day, we should note that Jacobs is not against planning per se; rather, she tentatively suggests that different planning approaches are necessary. Less clear, though, in her conception of the city, is what communities might do to plan for and secure large-scale changes – extending the city into the suburbs and beyond to accommodate population growth, renewing what no longer works, or shifting the city's form so that it can respond to the needs of a new age. For all the criticisms of Moses, the new highways, parkland and public amenity projects he led were intended to save the city from obsolescence. In his words, 'We are rebuilding New York, not dispersing and abandoning it.'

The notion that people might be well served by a comprehensive change in circumstances, planned or otherwise, is off the agenda today. Indeed, the very idea of comprehensive change is less likely today to be accepted as a means of improvement than to create fears over the potential disruption to community life. In such circumstances stability rather than change becomes attractive, and in the process helps create incentives and arguments for resisting development. In these circumstances, it is difficult to see how a planned city might be brought into existence in the UK today, or even how an existing conurbation might be re-planned in any way that moves beyond tinkering.

Given that we can all think of many successful places where no collaborative planning has been undertaken, one question that needs answering is why the activity of engaging the public should be any better at providing solutions to urban problems than large-scale planning? On the face of it, one might consider that engagement would offer fine-grained insights capable of informing plan-making, thereby enabling city design to respond more effectively to public needs and aspirations. However, collaborative planners suggest that there is a more profound reason why their methods make good sense. The answer, for them, lies in the distinctive approach to power embodied in the practice. Professor Tore Sager provides an illuminating definition for 'communicative planning': 'Making planning processes less vulnerable to manipulation and other repressive power strategies by revealing and counteracting communicative distortions. Aiming for broad participation and dialogue in planning processes and broad support for planning recommendations.'[30] This definition expresses the central case for the new approach – namely, that governments are intensely sensitive to their disconnection from the public, and to the suspicion of the public towards those in power. The act and quality of communication are perceived as critical to building good cities, because governments view planning as being about gaining new connections to the public. The planner is now a community facilitator, involved in the brokering and management of consent. This is what the UK's Conservative government calls 'community organisers': 'ground-up' trained 'activists' who have been funded by the state.[31]

Thus, communicative planning is a 'powerful conception in legitimising a managerialist approach to the problems confronting a planner'.[32] Christopher Bengs[33] also notes the degraded character of political community implicit in the change from the concept of the citizen to that of the stakeholder. The political community in collaborative planning theory is not the formal constituency of the electorate, but rather an informal constellation of voices – associated with a diverse, rather than universal, conception of the urbanite.

Jacobs came to prominence out of the protest movements that valued recourse to intervention in civic society through popular protest and direct action, rather than through the established channels of representative democracy. Today, the damaging implications of her propositions have been realised. Instead of thinking big and seeking democratic support, collaborative planning, and ideas about bottom-up change, actually sideline democracy. They focus on the process, rather than on what to build. Fermenting real change has become less important than engaging people in a dialogue.

CAN WE HAVE OUR PUBLIC BACK PLEASE?

Jacobs's proposition, made 50 years ago, appeared to rescue city planning both from the sterility of zoning and from the distance of the bureaucracy from the real lives of people. However, despite a commitment to dialogue, that distance has not been breached. Indeed, between then and now, the distance between people and politicians has massively increased. The political class today therefore has a much narrower social base.

The missing element in such an equation is the notion of the democratic will of the people, expressed in representative democracy. Most planners believe that people should be involved in planning through dialogue. Dialogue with people might be cynical if there are no choices to be made; but engaging people in real choices about places is otherwise a self-evidently good thing.

However, representative democracy responds to other opportunities. First, politicians have the potential to direct government, for example by marshalling resources for investment in infrastructure and development. Second, politicians are in a position to express the democratic will by determining what should happen: selecting one option over another where conflict exists. In this way, argument and conflict can play an important part in clarifying differences and informing choices. For all of its problems, post-war house-building in its many forms, from the Garden City style to Modernism, represented a response by government to the social needs of large sections of the population. It tells us much about the times we live in today that Robert Moses offends us: after all, bureaucrats are easy to control and direct if people and politics are strong; they appear powerful and manipulative if the public is absent from the stage.

Today, grand ambitions for cities do not enjoy wide support. But the will of the people is not well served if we do not make the case for the growth and transformation of our cities where we believe it to be necessary. Unlike Robert Moses and Baron Haussmann, we should seek to expose plans to the test of decision in public. But shrinking from the ambition for change, retreating from applying technological possibilities where they exist, failing to consider options that involve overriding one set of interests in favour of a greater good – none of this will serve people well.

The public must look to the political process, rather than to planning, as the place where this contestation is played out. The role for planners – those of us who want to make plans as opposed to spending our lives meandering through a marshland of policies designed to prevent development – is to present good ideas that can fuel political and public debate. Make No Little Plans!

NOTES

1.   Charles Moore, *Daniel H. Burnham, Architect, Planner of Cities*, vol. 2, Houghton Mifflin, 1921.

2. Richard Sennett, 'The Open City', *Urban Age* November 2006, at <www.urban-age.net/0_downloads/Berlin_Richard_Sennett_2006-The_Open_City.pdf>.
3. Alan Hudson, 'The Trouble with Planners', in Ian Abley and James Heartfield, *Sustaining Architecture in the Anti-Machine Age*, John Wiley & Sons, 2001, pp. 114–20.
4. Colin Ward, *Cotters and Squatters: The Hidden History of Housing*, Five Leaves Publications, 2002.
5. Colin Ward, 'The hidden history of housing', *History & Policy*, September 2004, at <www.historyandpolicy.org/papers/policy-paper-25.html>.
6. Lewis Mumford, *The City in History*, Penguin, 1966, p. 647.
7. Ibid., p. 114
8. James Holston, *The Modernist City*, Chicago and London: University of Chicago Press, 1989, p. 125.
9. Jürgen Habermas, *The Structural Transformation of the Public Sphere*, Polity Press, 1989.
10. Arendt quoted in ibid., p. 19.
11. Gordon E. Cherry, *Town Planning in Britain since 1900*, Blackwell, 1996.
12. Richard Sennett, *Flesh and Stone*, Faber & Faber, 1996, pp. 329–32.
13. 'Stop Pathfinder Demolition Call in Liverpool', *Brownfield Briefing*, 20 December 2010, at <www.brownfieldbriefing.com/news/stop-pathfinder-demolition-call-liverpool>.
14. Ebenezer Howard, *To-Morrow: A Peaceful Path to Real Reform*, 1898, in P. Hall, D. Hardy, E. Howard and C. Ward, *To-Morrow: A Peaceful Path to Real Reform*, Routledge, 2003.
15. Rhodri Windsor-Liscombe, 'Transcendent Modernity', in Iain Boyd Whyte, ed., *Modernism and the Spirit of the City*, Routledge, 2003, p. 188.
16. John Henry Forshaw and Patrick Abercrombie, *County of London Plan*, Macmillan, 1943.
17. Gordon E. Cherry, *Town Planning in Britain Since 1900*, Blackwell, 1996, p. 42.
18. Eric Mumford, *The CIAM Discourse on Urbanism, 1928–1960*, MIT Press, 2000.
19. Quoted in Windsor-Liscombe, 'Transcendent Modernity', p. 181.

20. Holston, *Modernist City*, University of Chicago Press, 1989.

21. Richard J. Williams, 'Oscar Niemeyer: Brasilia', *Blueprint*, February 2008.

22. Cees Nooteboom, 'Ex Nihilo: A Tale of Two Cities', in Iwan Baan, *Brasilia-Chandigargh*, Lars Muller Publishers, 2010.

23. Leonie Sandercock, *Towards Cosmopolis*, John Wiley & Sons, 1998, p. 24.

24. Hilary Ballon and Kenneth T. Jackson, eds, *Robert Moses and the Modern City: The Transformation of New York*, Norton, 2007.

25. Leonie Sandercock, *Cosmopolis II: Mongrel Cities in the 21st Century*, Continuum, 2003, p. 33.

26. Jane Jacobs, *The Death and Life of Great American Cities*, Penguin, 1961, p. 5.

27. John Gillot and Manjit Kumar, *Science and the Retreat from Reason*, Merlin Press, 1995.

28. Ralph Brand and Frank Gaffikin, 'Collaborative Planning in an Uncollaborative World', *Planning Theory* 6: 3 (November 2007), pp. 282–313.

29. Conservative Green Paper, 'Open Source Planning', 2010.

30. Tore Sager, 'Communicative Planners as Naïve Mandarins of the Neo-liberal State?', *European Journal of Spatial Development*, December 2005, p. 2.

31. Ben Glaze, 'Big Society Community Organisers to Get £20,000', *Independent*, 19 February 2011.

32. Sager, 'Communicative Planners as Naïve Mandarins of the Neo-liberal State?'.

33. Christopher Bengs, 'Planning Theory for the Naive', *European Journal of Spatial Development*, July 2005.

5
The Historic City
False Urban Memory Syndrome

Steve Nash and Austin Williams

They that reverence too much old times are but a scorn to the new.

Francis Bacon, 'Essays, Civil and Moral'

In the UK the heritage industry plays an important role in society. Led by well-known organisations such as the National Trust and English Heritage, it conjures up images of Stonehenge, of old stately homes and nature reserves, all preened and protected for the nation. In fact, woodland and monuments aside, there has been an almost exponential growth in the official rate of preservation orders and listing of buildings in the UK. Today there are 530,000 listed buildings across England and Wales – 'twice as many as in 1980 and three times as many as in 1970'.[1]

One such is the Park Hill housing estate in Sheffield. Said to have been inspired by Le Corbusier's Unité d'Habitation, it became Europe's largest listed building in 1998. Then arts minister Alan Howarth explained that it should be preserved to avoid the 'risk that it will be lost before its true value can be appreciated'.[2] Part of that value, as Stephen Bayley wryly observed, is an invention, whereby 'the security industry guards the fabric of tangible buildings, [while] heritage also looks after intangible national memory'.[3] But, for many, it was not a happy memory. After all, in Channel 4's *Demolition* programme in 2005, Park Hill made the list of the top twelve buildings that the public would most like to see torn down. But no matter: Park Hill, emblematic of the Modernist rejection of the past, is to be preserved for future generations as a reminder of 'the community spirit of traditional slum streets'.[4] What a tragic commemoration. As Le Corbusier said of his own profession, 'There is one profession and only one, architecture, in which progress is not considered necessary, where laziness is enthroned, and in which the reference is always to yesterday.'[5] We want to examine this reference to yesterday, when all our troubles seemed so far away. Hopefully, this chapter relates to more than just the architectural profession.

There are now 850 blue plaques on London buildings, commemorating a link between the building and a person who lived or worked there. They can undoubtedly offer some useful insights into the history of the city for tourists and inhabitants alike, and according to English Heritage, which administers the scheme, 'plaques bring buildings to life, showing us the places where important people in history lived and worked, demonstrating the capital's remarkable historical significance and uniting the past and present'.[6] For English Heritage, something of the person is lost when the physical building associated with them is demolished.

For some civic groups, however, the official plaques do not go far enough, and there have been demands for newer and more wide-ranging awards. For the Southwark Heritage Association,[7] the criteria applied by English Heritage – that plaques can only be placed on existing buildings, and that the person being commemorated must be deceased – were too restrictive. In their subversive scheme, launched in December 2002, one of the first plaques to be unveiled was for Sir Michael Caine, born in St Olave's Hospital in Rotherhithe in 1933, and very much alive. Not only that, but the building had been demolished. Nevertheless, in October 2003 a plaque was duly unveiled on the site, which now happens to be the home of a modern office block.

A heightened awareness of the past is symptomatic of those with little or no future. Pensioners or the terminally ill are at liberty to reminisce, but the fact that the country is engaged in the equivalent of looking back to the good old days is a little tragic, and is worth exploring more fully. We can all have opinions on which buildings and sites should be preserved, and which historic or popular figures should be commemorated; but it is our contention that a new sensibility about the past is being cultivated. We explore here where this has come from and how it works in practice. We also examine what, if anything, it tells us about ourselves.

URBAN MEMORY THEORY

Alongside the heritage industry, the 'urban memory' industry has established itself in recent years. Largely driven by academic papers and conferences, the last decade or so has witnessed a flowering of memory and identity as objects of public attention. Combined with the present political trends that fetishise therapy, well-being and happiness, a new sensibility is being actively cultivated in which the past is seen as a comfort blanket. Failing to remember who we are and where we come from is thought to be at the root of social disaggregation. This sense of social loss is most profoundly felt in the aging economies of the West, but even emerging societies like China are learning the language of self-enforced despair, one Chinese academic stating that 'today's changeable architecture and its environment destroy the familiar narrative context for residents, threaten and distort urban memory for next generations. Cities are unable to be the familiar home in people's memory any more, causing "social amnesia" eventually.'[8] Another writer suggests that 'the making of memory is a creative process engaged in an active dialogue with the past, moving beyond a present interpretation of it, as a comprehensive inventory of things past'.[9]

As far back as the early 20th century, urban analyst Walter Benjamin wrote of the tendency for memories to be unpredictable and, above all, unconscious: often sparked off by the most anodyne of stimuli. So is there any merit in attempting to develop a theory of how these individual responses – randomly triggered in the urban environment – can be understood and generalised to society at large?

The aim of the urban memory industry is to provide people with roots and to build a sense of belonging. Not only are we encouraged to preserve and conserve; we are also encouraged to feel an emotional attachment to places and periods from the past. By engaging with public urban memories, we are said to be developing an understanding of our locale; more importantly, however, such engagement is meant to cultivate self-reflection. With architects and urban designers being asked to take account of urban memories, we have arrived at a point where people's personal and emotional feelings about their surroundings are exerting an influence on the very fabric of the city.

THE CHANGING FACE OF LOCALISM

Arising from the globalisation debates over the last 20 years, an interest in urban memory has developed to counter the apparent shrinking of time and space, and to help us to feel rooted in a rapidly changing world. As the social geographer David Harvey explains, 'urbanization and the connectivity of urban places through networking across space are indeed changing very rapidly through the use of information technology'.[10] This change is said to have given rise to homogeneous towns and cities where history and memory are erased, and where citizens conform to the dictates of the world market. Those who celebrate locality paint a vivid picture of an isolated and vulnerable individual operating in a world where they are cut off from their cultural and historical roots. One could argue that there is nothing new in this cautious or fearful response to change. David Blunkett, former education minister in the Labour administration of the 1990s, asserted that 'familiar certainties and old ways of doing things are fast disappearing'.[11] Many have pointed out that globalisation and its effects have been with us ever since the creation of the world market in the nineteenth century. Tom Standage argues in *The Victorian Internet*[12] that the effect of telegraphy had a more far-reaching impact on nineteenth-century society in shrinking time and space than the Internet has had on modern society. This example might be a trifle hyperbolic, but that should not distract us from the fact that change is commonplace, and should be welcomed.

However, this chapter suggests that there is something different about the response to changing circumstances today compared to the past. A therapeutic ethos has colonised many of the institutions of society, and it is in this context that urban memory has begun to gain influence. Whether in education, with its obsession with self-esteem, or through government public health campaigns, state institutions have been reorientated towards a more therapeutic role. Lately, UK prime minister, David Cameron, has articulated a desire to change the economic remit of government to reflect this change. Speaking in 2006, he claimed that 'it's time we admitted that there's more to life than money and its time we focused not just on GDP, but on GWB – general well-being'. He went on to say that 'Well-being can't be measured by money or traded in markets. It's about the beauty of our surroundings, the quality of our culture and, above all, the strength of our relationships.'[13] Happiness and well-being are the new buzz words of the political elite across Europe as they try to redefine the purpose of government. It is in this context that urban memories are now having their effect. From the perspective of the urban memory advocates,

> we are currently witnessing the revalorization of individual and collective memory at a time when historical amnesia appears to be at an all time high. Many are searching for and building places of memory that can provide a sense of 'temporal anchoring' in a world of up-to-the-minute media saturation and 'information overload'.[14]

The imperative here is to fill the perceived inner psychological voids of the individual, rather than fulfil any wider social or political aspirations.

The philosopher Alain de Botton explains how the colourful context of urban memory is meant to work. Citing John Ruskin's romantic advocacy of 'word painting' – i.e. putting a visual experience into words as an exercise in a conscious appreciation and contemplative examination of one's surroundings – Ruskin, he says, 'recognised that many places strike us as beautiful not on the basis of aesthetic criteria … but on the basis of psychological criteria, because they embody a value or mood of importance to us'.[15] In contrast to Ruskin's rather innocent and benign conjecture on our relationship with the past, today's advocates of urban memory are more concerned with objective measures. For instance in designing a building to house John Ruskin's work and his library, Richard MacCormac was prompted to 'reflect on the relationship between the different languages of "modernism" and historical tradition, and how the past must not just be preserved, but made part of the future'.[16] So should we celebrate urban memories, preserving our locality and our past? Or should we reject the past as a way of looking to the future, by turning outwards and understanding the world? Might there be a happy balance between these two positions?

MODERN MAN

Le Corbusier advanced the idea that 'movement is the law of our existence: nothing ever stands still'.[17] Today, this sense that the past needs to be swept away in order to make a fresh start is not widely felt. Rather, we live in an anxious age – one in which there is a feeling that too much of the past has been rejected and that, as a consequence, we are living in an era without moral or intellectual guidance. The conservative philosopher Roger Scruton makes the point that 'in architecture and literature we find the same story, of art at war with its past, forced to challenge the rule of clichés, and to set off on a path of transgression'.[18] According to Scruton this transgression has left us rudderless and without reference points with which to navigate our way around the world. We are, it is said, unclear on what lessons we can learn from the past, and consequently nervous about the future. The search for urban memories with which to 'anchor' ourselves in the world is taking place in a world that lacks confidence and belief in its own bigger story.

Many writers have recognised the dilemma. In 1982, Marshall Berman mused on those who were grappling with the issues of modernity, describing them as 'moved at once by a will to change – to transform both themselves and their world – and by a terror of disorientation and disintegration, of life falling apart. They all know the thrill and dread of a world in which "all that is solid melts into air".'[19]

Sadly, for today's writers the thrill has gone and only the dread remains. Jonathan Franzen's book *Freedom* has been referred to as a 'great American novel' by many reviewers, and has obviously struck a chord with liberal America. Framing the novel within a Malthusian fear of too many people, he suggests that we suffer from too much freedom or too many liberties. Chiming with the contemporary anxiety about the 'paralysing problem of too many choices'[20] it is common to hear arguments for limits, not only in terms of population growth but also in terms of people's lives. For Franzen, it seems, people need solid, anchored, simple references so that they can know themselves and the world.[21] Similarly in architecture, there are those who want to root their work in place and memory in order to provide clear references and meaning for people. This 'building memory' has been described as

> the sum of all the traces in the city but likewise if development sweeps buildings away then memory loss and identity crisis threaten and the city loses its typology (its memory forms), and can no longer act as a kind of guide or exemplar for the people living in it.[22]

Many architects and urbanists now trying to find ways of reconciling historic and contemporary design seem keenly aware of Scruton's criticism, and wish to incorporate the past within their work. These 'mirrors of our identity', as Milan Kundera described them,[23] reconfigure the aforementioned dilemma and, we would argue, are representative of a malaise. We are being invited to believe that this incorporation of scattered memories within the building is providing us with a sense of place and of belonging. However, surely a sense of meaning and of place is not going to be created by architects, but has to happen as a political project in the wider society. The substitution of urban design or architecture for politics over-flatters the power of design and underplays the necessity of political intervention.

MEMORIES REINTERPRETED

Some insist that the benefits of incorporating memory within the built environment are based upon science; neuroscience in general, social science in particular, but actually pseudo-science in essence. In December 2010 the Abbey Road zebra crossing in London achieved Grade II listed status. The crossing is, of course, famous for appearing on the cover of a Beatles album that shares the name of the road. As John Penrose, the minister for tourism and heritage, explained, 'This London zebra crossing is no castle or cathedral, but thanks to the Beatles and a ten-minute photo shoot one August morning in 1969, it has just as strong a claim as any to be seen to be part of our heritage.'[24] That tourists love to have their photographs taken on the crossing while trying to recreate the iconic Beatles cover illustrates something of the psychology at work. For the urban memory theorist, this qualifies as an instance of *lieux de memoire*, or 'place of memory', in which the crossing can trigger memories of the past. In this context, the practical function of the crossing is secondary to the memory-triggering role it is seen to play.

These 'triggers' are similar to Proust's involuntary memories. The sensory experience seems to take the person back in time, so that the memory of the past really does come alive. This is not just a conscious act of remembering, but a psychosomatic reaction to a place, and the response cannot be allied purely to the location; it is as much governed by time, mood, dreams and ambition as it is by physically real past experiences. Perhaps the person on the zebra crossing is reliving the happy memories of their youth, when a new Beatles album had just been released. Another might recall when they were almost run over on a zebra crossing. For others, the whole experience will simply amount to parentally induced embarrassment. It is clear that, whatever the outcome, the emotional reality for the person concerned is palpable. But we have no way of capturing the definitive cause–effect relationship that is induced – or fails to be induced – by a place, because of the multitude of subjective elements at play.

For the urban memory theorist, what occurs can be set against the simple nostalgia that we associate with the heritage industry. We are not being encouraged to live in the past; rather we are being invited to live in the here-and-now, but fortified by the emotional attachment that urban memories provide. Generalised responses are all that can be offered, but this subjective psychological phenomenon has had an increasing influence on decisions around urban design.

Used until recently as an out-patient annexe for the Middlesex Hospital in London, a building due for demolition has become the focus of a campaign to prevent its redevelopment for new housing. Unbeknown to many of those who have used the building, it was erected in 1778 as a parish poorhouse, known as the Strand Union workhouse. It is this connection that campaigners wish to preserve. Research has uncovered that, in his youth, Charles Dickens lived nearby and may have been aware of the institution and its grimly necessary purpose. It is surmised, although we can never know for sure, that the workhouse featured in Oliver Twist, which is one of the reasons for its preservation. The non-fictional medical officer attached to it at the time, Dr Joseph Rogers, was a reformist who campaigned against the appallingly cramped, squalid conditions in the area. He is said to have despised the building, and would presumably have welcomed its demolition back in his day. Some have noted this irony. The local MP, Frank Dobson, commented on the campaign to save the collection of buildings: 'It seems unlikely that [Rogers] would be flattered to have them retained, particularly at the expense of new affordable housing.'[25] The perceived need to preserve urban memories does not always meet with unanimous support, especially when it comes up against issues of housing need in the here-and-now. For the campaigners, however, 'its preservation would be a fitting testament to so many of the nation's poor whose lives were dominated by the poor law system right up until the foundation of the National Health Service in 1948'.[26]

This is the collective memory syndrome. On one hand, there is an assumption that there is a magical power within construction that evokes a truth – an essence of a national collective identity. Places like Buckingham Palace, Downing Street, the Millennium Dome, and so on, have indeed encapsulated something about the nation; but all of these commemorate something real: they are reflective of social reality, rather than creating it. Whether it is deference to the monarchy, or the contentlessness of the Dome, each of these edifices articulates a truth about British national culture – whether post-war exuberance, dead-end Britain, or something else again. Collective memory becomes a building's frame of reference, capturing a momentary mood which, for some people, becomes the defining characteristic of that building.

On the other hand, the collective memory narrative is more than a personal, private experience; and it is also not simply the tangible reflection of a pre-existing mood or historical moment. It is a mantra that now seeks to re-forge – in fact to create – a sense of the collective. The main problem with the debate today is that our individualised responses to places and *objets trouvés* are being squeezed into a policy framework which, instead of trying to improve the physical environment in a tangible way, is seeking to generate an intangible urban feel-good factor. This is an industry set up to create a link with the past even if that link is to something that has formerly gone unnoticed. Rarely are memories self-creating; increasingly it is the case that they are revived for us by researchers and campaigners, not by the community itself.

Nowadays, while we have 'valid' memories, we also have the creation of 'inappropriate' memories. Belfast's Shipyard Memorial Wall, for example depicts the 'rich heritage' of the Harland and Wolff site that built the *Titanic* nearly a century ago. Ten years ago, locals were being encouraged to tie to the wall pictures of objects representing a personal memory of the site, which were intended to 'make a mark' – to create a sense of place and purpose – on behalf of the community. Real memory is being manipulated through such vacuous performances, expressed in the fact that hostile, antagonistic or partisan memorabilia – the essence of the shipyard's (and the city's) troubled history – are not permitted in this exhibition. It seems that this is the latest in a long line of urban memorials that airbrush the true 'rich heritage' of sectarianism out of the history of the area. This device also provides a managed route for emotional outpouring as a cover for the inevitable redundancies. Not surprisingly, city officials are happy to see the Samson and Goliath gantry cranes becoming city landmarks, ensuring that pride rather than anger becomes the governing emotion.

The imposition of an agenda is sometimes more subtle. In Berlin, memory is valid only when it is contrite. It seems as if the Second World War and the Cold War are the only frames of reference for a legitimate memory experience in that city. As one paper gleefully suggested at the turn of the millennium, 'At last, the Holocaust and the Second World War seemed to have become an integral part of German national identity.'[27] Peter Eisenman, the architect of the Memorial to the Murdered Jews of Europe, bases much of his work on the concept of *Sehnsucht* – the unrealisable desire or inconsolable longing contained in the 'haunting' memory of narrative structures.[28]

In fact, as Nietzsche observed, it would be 'altogether impossible to live at all without forgetting'.[29] But often this instinctive necessity is denied to us. South Africa's Truth and Reconciliation Commission, for instance, is still a major reference point. Despite the words of Archbishop Desmond Tutu: '[H]aving asked and received forgiveness and having made amends, let us shut the door on the past – not in order to forget it but in order not to allow it to imprison us',[30] the past still forms an all-encompassing frame of reference for the country. In his excellent book, *Ways of Staying*, South African author Kevin Bloom captures the ironic predicament of a man who was too young to have played any active part in apartheid, but who – almost by force of circumstances – still has to define his life through its prism.

In the UK, the Institute of Public Policy Research, a Labourite think-tank, has long explored 'the role of design in promoting democratic engagement', and launched a Town Hall competition on the basis that '[t]own halls are the public face of local councils. Yet … few speak the language of our informal, democratic times. The aim of the Designs on Democracy competition was to encourage designers to explore ways in which town halls might be transformed into lively centres of political and civic life.'[31] Such instrumentalism, which asserts that constructing civic architecture can reformulate civic engagement, is crass in the extreme. It also wilfully fails to engage with the deeper problem of why there is disengagement in the first place.

NON-COLLECTIVE AUTHORITY

After the Second World War, 150,000 prefabricated houses were built in the UK. One of the last of these estates still remains in Catford, South London. Built by German prisoners of war in 1946–47, the Excalibur estate is now under threat of demolition due to its poor state of repair. Prefabs, as they are known, were built as temporary homes due to the post-war housing shortage, so it is a testament to their design that some are still standing 60 years later. The process of change and of re-housing the residents has been fraught with difficulty. Understandably, for some of the older residents it is a time of emotional upset – a not unfamiliar situation for many leaving their homes of long standing later in life when so many memories and attachments are embodied in them. However, the 187 homes on the Excalibur estate have become more than just a re-housing issue. For the advocates of urban memory, the prefabs need to be preserved because they evoke a working-class culture of the past that needs to be remembered by the present generation. For the commentator Simon Jenkins, 'The prefab estate is a small piece of working-class history, no less worthy for not being conventionally beautiful.'[32]

The prefabs themselves are seen as places of collective memory. It is this emotional attachment that is being protected alongside the physical structures. This is not just an example of conservation, but part of a wider social policy agenda that sees the past as a means of cementing communities together. In fact, the residents themselves seemed split on what to do for the best. Eventually a majority voted to accept Lewisham Council's decision to rebuild, causing English Heritage to list six of the houses. One of the residents is quoted as saying, 'A lot of people now are really getting fed up. The people that wanted listed buildings should go and live in them. In five or six years' time we'll all be sitting in our nice and cosy new houses while theirs are falling down around their ears.'[33] This highlights one of the central problems with collective urban memory: it isn't actually collective.

Stemming from the heritage industry's rationale to recreate a sense, not of place, but of experience, urban memory is all about an intuitive relationship to events. One problem with it, among many, is that it demotes a rational and contextualised understanding of place-making history – of actions and consequences – and replaces it with a celebration of the spontaneity of the moment, of the natural, of the 'relevant'.

Ironically, many people would prefer to put the past behind them than to be continually reminded of it. Perhaps the people living in a community intuitively understand that communities are in a state of flux, and that nothing remains the same forever. Do people place the same significance on their day-to-day surroundings that the academics, theorists and intervening activists claim?

THE ROLE OF SELF

The UK has produced some eminent writers who are fascinated with the psychology of place. Peter Ackroyd, Iain Sinclair and Will Self have created a whole genre of work about the relationship of people to places. Whether it is Iain Sinclair walking around the M25 or Will Self walking to an airport, their interest is in exploring areas that are off the beaten track, both geographically and psychologically. For instance, Self believes that by walking to and from airports he is able to overcome the 'compromised reality' of those who catch buses and trains to and from the airport.

These unelected spokesmen for the collective (for the community, for the nation), are less interested in being seen as men about town than in not being seen at all as they traverse the soulless spaces between towns. It says something about our culture that this fascination with the obscure and with out-of-the-way places should make these itinerants into the exemplars of the Everyman. In their work the city becomes personified, and its personality always seems to be a troubled and disconcerting one. Iain Sinclair likes to explore the hidden backwaters of our post-industrial world. In his book *Edge of the Orison*,[34] for instance, he traces the journey of the poet John Clare from the lunatic asylum in Epping Forest back to his

home near Peterborough. These journeys are around or away
from the city.

Their work is a long way from the detachment of the nineteenth
century. Writers like Baudelaire in Paris and Dickens in London
were more concerned with developing a new way of seeing that
incorporated the modern world, rather than rejecting modernity
altogether. Paul Verlaine, writing of the influence of Baudelaire,
said that his

> originality is to portray, powerfully and originally, modern man ... as the
> refinements of an excessive civilisation have made him, modern man with
> his acute and vibrant senses, his painfully subtle spirit, his brain saturated
> with tobacco, his blood burning with alcohol ... Baudelaire portrays this
> sensitive individual as a type, a hero.[35]

One of Baudelaire's heroes was Balzac, precisely because he
engaged at such a profound level with the people. His art came
out of this relationship in the same way that Dickens's work
did. The greater the distance from this engagement, the greater
the tendency to ascribe meaning where there is none. So, for
example, Will Self may believe that Londoners do not live in
London but in a tube-map version of the city because they
lack his spatial awareness; but this tells us more about his own
alienation than it does about reality. Too much significance is
claimed for the trivial and the everyday, and this seems to have
rubbed off on architects and urban designers as well.

We have all become familiar with the claims made for the 2012
London Olympics. The Olympics are tasked with regenerating
east London in general and the inner-city borough of Newham
in particular. Newham Council is in no doubt that the games
'represent a once in a lifetime opportunity for us to raise the
profile of the borough, improve our transport networks and
inspire people to participate in sport and healthy lifestyles'.[36]
For those in authority and for the designers that they have
employed, the Games seem to be all about 'legacy' – what comes
afterwards, rather than the Games themselves. David Higgins,
chief executive of the Olympic Delivery Authority, has said that
the Olympics 'can be viewed as a sporting overlay for the biggest

regeneration project in Europe'.[37] With claims mounted for the present – from regeneration, to inspiring 'people to participate in sporting and healthy lifestyles' or to 'to raise aspirations, develop self esteem and confidence'[38] – the Games themselves have 'legacy' as a stated aim. That is to say, the ambition for the Olympics is the memory in the future of an event that has yet to take place.[39] As one London conference put it, 'The London 2012 Olympics are already providing memories and experiences for a lot of people, despite not yet being completed.'[40] The desire to embed experiences securely into the future surely reflects a fear of the unknown and a search for continuity.

Similarly, when new public spaces are built today they are tasked with unrealistic social objectives. The new development of Canada Water, in south-east London, has taken ten years to come to fruition. For the residents, the attraction has been the new transport links and the large shopping centre; but for the local authority and the designers the priority has been creating a new sense of place for these residents. The focus of the development will be a public space to be known as Deal Porter Plaza, in 'memory of the thousands of workers in the area employed as porters to carry the deal wood arriving in the old Surrey Docks from Canada'.[41] Resting on the edge of the dock basin, Canada Water library is also intended to provide a focus for the community: a unique sense of place for new and existing residents. Both the square and the library are tasked with something far greater than their outward functions: they are to bring people together and generate new community awareness. The problem is that this community togetherness is a top-down construction, and one suspects that the public will need to conform to what the local authority expects of a community when using the public square. Reflecting on the rise of new 'civic' buildings and *grands projets*, urban geographer Katharyne Mitchell notes that, 'in the attempt to harness nostalgia and foster a sense of collective memory … the development of museums and anchoring institutions … all help[s] to sanitise spaces and provide an image of enjoyable leisure and endless present'.[42] The attempt to foster a 'sense of collective memory' can have the effect of freezing society in an endless present, which can mean

The Book Depository

Free Delivery Worldwide

5
4
3
2
1

6
5
4
3
2
1

0 CM Ruler INCHES 0

Book Depository
Free Delivery Worldwide

6'8								2
6'7								2
6'6								1
6'5								1
6'4								1
6'3								1
6'2								1
6'1								1
6'0								1
5'11								1
5'10								1
5'9								1
5'8								1
5'7								1
5'6								1
5'5								1
5'4								1
5'3								1
5'2								1
5'1								1
5'0								1
4'11								1
4'10								1
4'9								1
4'8								

Feet to metres

societal stagnation. Everything becomes sanitised in this world, so that any conflicting perspectives are ironed out, leaving us with an enforced consensus. The real means by which urbanity occurs – through actions and their consequences – are sidelined, leaving behind merely an artificial construct.

The contemporary fetish for urban memory is all about celebrating an intuitive relationship to your locality. It is as if we are all being called upon endlessly to seek, but never quite reach, our destination. Collective urban memories are an extension of the project of embedding socially correct values through the urban fabric, rather than through democratic discourse. We need to reassert the need for a rational and contextualised understanding of place-making history – of actions and consequences – if we are to reassemble genuine urbanity. Memories have their place, but sometimes we have to be allowed to reject or rise above them.

Admittedly, there is no intrinsic harm in referencing the past – there is nothing to be gained by wilful philistinism, prejudice or ignorance. But we can, and should, challenge and reject the social policy-driven false memories that now masquerade as our own remembrances. There is an urgent need to recognise that, when we ask what the urban future holds, we seldom find answers in the past.

NOTES

1. James Heartfield, *Let's Build!*, Audacity, 2006, p. 51.
2. BBC News, 'UK Housing Estates Get Listed Status', 23 December 1998, at <www.news.bbc.co.uk/2/hi/uk_news/241650.stm>.
3. Stephen Bayley, 'The Muddled Magic Kingdom That Is English Heritage', *Observer*, 19 April 2009.
4. English Heritage listing quoted in Richard Marsden, 'Park Hill Flat Mates – What Should Happen Now?', *Sheffield Star*, 1 October 2009.
5. 'Art: Corbusierismus', *Time*, 4 November 1935, at <www.time.com/time/magazine/article/0,9171,755279,00.html>.
6. English Heritage, 'Blue Plaques: About This Scheme', at <www.english-heritage.org.uk/discover/blue-plaques/about>.

7. Southwark Heritage, 'Southwark Heritage Blue Plaque Scheme', at <www.squidoo.com/Southwark-Heritage-Blue-Plaque-Scheme>.

8. Zhu Rong, 'The Contemporary Challenge: Urban Conservation Issues in Present-Day China', paper delivered at *Mirror Of Modernity: The Post-war Revolution in Urban Conservation*, joint conference convened by DOCOMOMO-International and the Architectural Heritage Society of Scotland, 1–2 May 2009.

9. Federica Goffi, 'The Sempiternal Nature of Architectural Conservation and the Unfinished Building and Drawing', PhD thesis, Virginia Polytechnic Institute and State University, 2010, p. 205.

10. D. Harvey, 'Megacities Lecture 4', p. 32, at <www.megacities.nl/lecture_4/possible.pdf>.

11. David Blunkett quoted in Frank Furedi, 'Re-reading C. P. Snow and His Elusive Search for Authority', in Robert Whelan, ed., *From Two Cultures to No Culture*, Civitas, 2009, p. 71.

12. Tom Standage, *The Victorian Internet*, Weidenfeld & Nicholson, 1998, pp. 188–98.

13. BBC News, 'Make People Happier, Says Cameron', 22 May 2006, at <www.news.bbc.co.uk/1/hi/uk_politics/5003314>.

14. R. Rose-Redwood, D. Alderman and M Azaryahu, 'Collective Memory and the Politics of Urban Space: An Introduction', *GeoJournal* 73: 3, pp. 160–3.

15. Alain de Botton, 'The Art of Travel', Penguin, 2003, p. 234.

16. Richard MacCormac, 'Architecture, Memory and Metaphor', *Architectural Review*, November 1996, at <www.findarticles.com/p/articles/mi_m3575/is_n1197_v200/ai_19018109/?tag=content;col1pp.1l>.

17. Le Corbusier, *Towards a New Architecture*, Architectural Press, 1923.

18. Roger Scruton, *Beauty*, Oxford University Press, 2009.

19. Marshall Berman, *All That Is Solid Melts Into Air*, Verso, 1982, pp. 13, 132.

20. Alina Tugend, 'Too Many Choices: A Problem That Can Paralyze', *New York Times*, 26 February 2010.

21. Jonathan Franzen, *Freedom*, Farrar, Straus & Giroux, 2010.

22. Mark Crinson, 'Urban Memory: An Introduction', in Mark Crinson, ed., *Urban Memory: History and Amnesia in the Modern City*, Routledge, 2005, p. xiii.
23. Milan Kundera, *Identity*, HarperCollins, 1998.
24. Department for Culture, Media and Sport, '"And in the end…" the Abbey Road Zebra Crossing is "Listed" by Tourism and Heritage Minister John Penrose', press release, 22 December 2010, at <www.culture.gov.uk/news/media_releases/7683.aspx>.
25. R. Osley 'He Hated the Sight of It, So Why Save It in His Name?', *Camden New Journal*, 3 April 2008, at <www.thecnj.com/camden/2008/040308/news040308_14.html>.
26. Dickens Felllowship, 'Save the Cleveland Street Workhouse', at <www.dickensfellowship.org/save-cleveland-street-workhouse>.
27. R. Wittlinger, 'Collective Memory and National Identity in the Berlin Republic: The Emergence of a New Consensus?', *Debatte: Journal of Contemporary Central and Eastern Europe* 14: 3 (2006), p. 201.
28. Austin Williams, 'Nobody Needs Architecture', *Blueprint*, 2 December 2010.
29. Nietzsche quoted in Sergio Della Sala, ed., *Forgetting: Current Issues in Memory*, Hove & New York: Psychology Press, 2010, p. xiii.
30. Truth and Reconciliation Commission, 'TRC FINAL REPORT – Summary and Guide to Contents', 1995, vol. 1, chapter 1, para. 91.
31. Ben Rogers, 'Designs on Democracy – Winners Announced', IPPR, 20 January 2003, at <www.ippr.org.uk/pressreleases/archive.asp?id=679&fID=60>.
32. Simon Jenkins, 'Excalibur's Castles Built from Postwar Dreams Must Not Be Demolished', *Guardian*, 6 January 2011, at <www.guardian.co.uk/commentisfree/2011/jan/06/excalibur-castles-prefab-post-war-demolished>.
33. *News Shopper*, 'CATFORD: Prefabs Listed in Estate Threatened with Demolition', 18 March 2009, at <www.newsshopper.co.uk/news/4211511.CATFORD__Prefabs_listed_in_estate_threatened_with_demolition>.
34. Iain Sinclair, *Edge of the Orison*, London: Penguin, 2005.
35. Berman, *All That Is Solid Melts Into Air*.

36. London Borough of Newham, 'Newham and the 2012 Games', press release, at <www.newham.gov.uk/2012Games/AboutThe2012Games/default.htm>.

37. David Higgins quoted in 'London 2012 can be the "Regeneration Games"', Olympic Delivery Authority press release, 22 November 2006.

38. Newham Council, *Newham and the 2012 Games*, 2009, at <www.newham.gov.uk/2012Games/AboutThe2012Games/default.htm>.

39. Cathy Smith, 'The Record: A Legacy for the London 2012 Olympic and Paralympic Games and the Cultural Olympiad', *National Archives*, British Library, November 2009.

40. Stella Jackson, 'Designating the Olympics: London 2012, a National Heritage Asset?', paper delivered at 'Heritage and the Olympics: 11th Cambridge Heritage Seminar', convened by the University of Cambridge, 24 June 2010.

41. Canada Water Regeneration with Southwark Council, 'Plaza', at <www.canadawater-southwark.co.uk/details/plaza>.

42. Katharyne Mitchell, 'The Culture of Urban Space', *Urban Geography* 21: 5 (1 July–15 August 2000), pp. 443–9, at <bellwether.metapress.com/content/5126622m21w17580/resource-secured/?target=fulltext.pdf>.

6
The Sanitised City
If You've Done Nothing Wrong…

Tony Pierce and Austin Williams

What a beautiful noise … It's the song of the cars …
Neil Diamond, 'What a Beautiful Noise'

William H. Whyte, the pioneer of urban research, made a renowned sociological movie, released in 1980, titled *The Social Life of Small Urban Spaces*.[1] In it, he studied the characteristics of behaviour of the public in eight plazas in downtown New York to explain why some were successful and others not. Research teams analyzed the movements of people as they used, or avoided, the public spaces that designers had created.

The edited documentary shows beautifully how people are the ones who make public space work. With the best intentions and valiant attempts of designers to make us do certain things, regularly we vehemently do the opposite. In the film, children see narrow ledges – designed to stop people using them – as challenges. Whyte's famous conclusion that 'people will sit where there are places to sit' is a truism that is still ignored by many urbanists, here exemplified by people using rolled up newspapers to sit on walls interspersed with spikes – the very spikes that had been placed there in order to prevent loitering by the 'undesirables'.

What was, and remains, striking is how sociable people were, and how much interaction went on between strangers, as well as friends and families. There was evidently considerable unspoken trust between individuals in 1970s New York. Nowadays, the young men in the film drinking alcohol, eyeing up the girls and blocking the thoroughfare would undoubtedly be frowned upon.

Unsupervised children would no longer be acceptable, as the police are within their rights, in the UK at the least, 'to remove under-16-year-olds to their place of residence between the hours of 9 p.m. and 6 a.m.',[2] regardless of whether any crime has been committed or commissioned.

Could such a film be made now? Possibly not; and not just because of the suspicion that would inevitably be cast on an elderly man with a telephoto lens secretly filming young women lounging in public squares, then logging their leisure habits and monitoring their movements. In the years since this movie – which celebrated the public use of public space and encouraged urban designers to manufacture spaces that might encourage such public participation – there has been a growing recognition that urban spaces have ceased to be truly social. Partly to blame are overregulation, surveillance (which played a minor walk-on part in Whyte's movie) and the plethora of bans and restrictions now in place. But the disaggregation of the Weberian concept of 'social action' and the fracturing of communality seems to have taken away our ability to act coherently as a public.

This chapter will examine the rise of authoritarian intervention and the consequent privatisation of the public sphere, concentrating primarily on the UK. Much has been written about the erosion of the public sphere by private interests (the replacement of public commons by private malls, for example), and so that does not provide the substance of the chapter. Its central theme is the general repudiation of the autonomous private citizen within the public sphere. This reflects the opposite trajectory to that of privatisation, pointing to the tendency of the public gaze to intrude upon the private. All too often, the motives of the private individual are deemed to be public property. Many people believe that this is nothing new, and so we also examine the differences in form and content between historic intrusions into individual choice 'for the public good' and the way that they manifest themselves today. We conclude with an appraisal and critique of the new policy mechanisms for generating social capital: the official attempts to remodel 'the new public' in the plaza.

UNEQUAL EQUITY

Unsurprisingly, life in big cities is often messy. The new Purple Flag award – similar to the Blue Flag scheme for standards on Britain's beaches – certificates cities that are safe, welcoming and enjoyable.[3] Ironically, flag-winning Manchester is also, apparently, the most violent city in the UK to live in.[4] One hundred and fifty years ago, one academic writer noted that New York's 'hurry' and 'bustle', and its constant noise, were all a vital part of the dynamism of life in the modern metropolis: 'It is contagious, and it has a good effect upon the spirits and health of an idle man.'[5]

Ed Hollis, author of *The Secret Lives of Buildings*, notes that 'public engagement in public spaces is a risky and threatening affair – and so it should be'.[6] Such are the contradictions of metropolitan life, to the extent that without them – without these polarised experiences – it would cease to be a city.

But this view might justifiably lay itself open to the charge of romantic blindness, as there is nothing attractive (to most people) about violence; about the real poverty, crime and unpleasantness that lurk beneath the surface of parts of our urban agglomerations. Whether in the form of homelessness, hunger, overcrowding or pollution, the struggle for the city's inequitably distributed resources can sometimes result in pain and discomfort.

In truth, however, the city is all about equity. American academic Edward Glaeser has done an admirable job in defending the progress of urban centres as an ugly, but necessary, stepping-stone out of poverty. Where some note that cities breed inequity, he points out that cities simply attract poor people, thus giving the appearance of a poverty trap. He makes a comparison with public transport in developing countries, where the poor need to congregate in close proximity to the railway lines because it is simply economically beneficial for them to do so. That, after all, is where necessary trade and transport lie for those unable to afford the luxury of distance. He defies anyone to suggest that public transport *causes* poverty, but notes that commentators are less circumspect about condemning cities for the same thing. Because few people become fabulously wealthy, the statistical imbalance of wealth is maintained; but poor people are reasonably adept, he asserts, in not staying poor.

It is an historical truism that run-down areas of cities are often prone to criminality, disease and high rates of mortality. Not just in under-developed countries, but in the West too, the life chances befalling the poor are worse than those for the rich. This may be unsurprising, but it is still disturbing. In a review of deaths in the UK between 1921 and 2007, inequality between the rich and the poor was shown to have increased. But a closer reading revealed that '[h]ealth in the most disadvantaged parts of the country is improving rapidly, but the *relative* gap is growing … the health of the most disadvantaged has not improved as quickly as that of the better off'. But it has significantly improved.

Make no mistake, this chapter is not intended as a defence of inequality, disease or death. It does not advocate anarchy or deny that law-breaking might need to be prosecuted. It does not suggest that violence and crime just represent the rough and tumble of modern city life. It merely points out that the elevation of these aspects of urban living in public consciousness alter the perceptions of what a city has to offer.

Indeed, public behaviour that might be offensive to some is often not to others. For example, public expressions of affection may be appropriate in one country, but not in another. Group animus may be more acceptable in one type of public space (the football ground), but not in another (the shopping mall). Taste also changes over time, so that what was acceptable in the past is sometimes no longer so. Frequently, misdemeanours are so minor that it is curious that their perpetrators are being pursued. All too often, amid the heightened fears about urban life, we find that the story does not really rest on behaviour and standards that are shaking society to the core. Crime is crime; but drink a can of lager on the Underground, smoke in a public place, or photograph a child, and you will feel the wrath of the authorities over crimes that are not really criminal acts.

Jaywalking, which is not yet an offence in the UK, has serious consequences in the US. Distinguished historian Felipe Fernández-Armesto tried to cross the road in Atlanta, while attending the

2007 conference of the American Historical Association, only
to find himself in handcuffs and surrounded by armed police. 'I
come from a country where you can cross the road where you
like', said the visiting professor of global environmental history
at Queen Mary college, University of London.[7] In fact, in the UK,
it is driving that is the suspect activity, with pedestrians given
(theoretical) priority on some roads and urban Home Zones
privileging the occasional road-crosser over the road-user.

You can smoke a joint in public in Amsterdam or San
Francisco and, so long as it has no tobacco in it, no one turns
their head. Do the same elsewhere in the world and you could
get yourself locked up. In UK cities, public movement is widely
recorded on CCTV, with over half a million surveillance cameras
estimated to be in use in London.[8] Yet start taking pictures of a
crowded street on your own camera and you excite the interest
of the authorities. Assembly of more than two people in a public
place in the UK, if considered a threat to public order, can lead
to arrest. In most European cities, however, promenading and
hanging out in large numbers in public spaces is still encouraged.

The last thirty years – the span of a generation – in the UK
have seen an explosion of bans, rules and regulations on urban
life, along with surveillance by cameras and officialdom. In 1980
there were thirteen acts of parliament recognisable as influencing
public behaviour, whereas in 2008 there were over 300 similar
pieces of legislation, and their rate has increased – even under
the coalition government with its determination to cut 'red
tape'. New regulations in Britain, ranging from traffic controls
to changes to flexible working rules, jumped by 45 per cent,
from 2,008 in 2009 to 2,926 in 2010. The total is the highest
since records began, in 1987.

There have, of course, always been social rules to be followed
in the public life of cities. Most great cities grew from frenetic
origins. The creation of generalised order from potential chaos
has always been central to civic organisation. Many past rules
were culturally and historically progressive, addressing universal
problems and the protection of public health; but city and
national governments, particularly in recent years, have targeted
an increasing number of individual behaviours for legislation

and enforcement. The tsunami of regulatory procedures in fact exemplifies a state not fully in control, and seeking out technical fixes and procedural niceties to assert its authority. It just wants, it seems, to 'connect'.

Reflecting cultural differences, some regulations are quirky in the extreme, especially when introduced to deal with exceptional circumstances or events. But behind many of them is a growing assumption by authorities of the role of managing and directing how we behave as individuals, and how we interact with each other. We believe that this should be of concern to all of us; but many will say it has ever been thus.

PAST VERSUS PRESENT

When criticising the increasing intrusion into private life – the restrictions on smoking in public, the congestion charge in London, and so on – some will say that the government's Clean Air Act of 1956 was similarly illiberal, but that it was a public health good. In instances like this, they say, the heavy hand of the state is necessary for the good of the public. But does the comparison stand up to scrutiny?

It is undoubtedly the case that city burghers and officials have always striven to establish principles of acceptable behaviour. Victorian by-laws ensured that urban housing in UK cities was built according to very specific and detailed codes, and Edwardian police were not averse to cuffing a few miscreants for being in the wrong place. But this chapter contends that there is a different mood and ambition behind contemporary curbs on behaviour.

Below we compare and contrast a few examples from the past with today, to explore the changed motivations for each.

Public Health Versus Private Lifestyle

Victorian society invented the notion of public health. A cholera epidemic of 1847 was closely followed by a Public Health Act in 1848, although its introduction probably had more to do with the government's need to respond to pressure from the

Chartist demonstrations around the country than with the epidemic. The Public Health Act 1875 was more comprehensive, incorporating regulations on housing, sewerage, water supplies, street lighting and pavements. This was a 'glorious success for the promoters of Chadwick's sanitary idea'.[9] The consequences of this legislation were improved housing and sanitary conditions for all city-dwellers. Its impacts were intended to be universal, benefiting everyone with improved water supplies, drainage and sewerage. Countless thousands of people lived longer as a result of this and other interventions to enforce standards of provision for the basics of life.

You could argue that stopping people throwing chamber pots into the street, or from defecating near water-courses, was intended to reduce harm and distress to others, which is all too often the rhetoric used today to impose restrictions on personal behaviour deemed to be a nuisance. One hundred years ago, however, there was an unmistakably expansive mindset reflected in the improved infrastructural opportunities to deal with real public health problems. The authorities did not necessarily seek to berate individuals for doing the only thing available to them, but instead sought to provide an improved quality of opportunity for all. Developing mains sewerage infrastructure was a terrific engineering achievement responding to genuine medical research into a devastating disease. Not so today, when limits are the order of the day. Minimising one's adverse impact on others is a moral obligation. Today, a comparable case study might compel people to use the toilet less often – to restrict use at source rather than to increase provision; indeed, the rise of the waterless composting toilet, unconnected to the mains, is regularly cited as a way of reducing the load on the system. But using water is not a harm. In fact, for most people, using it is a sign of civilised behaviour. But the contemporary attitude is that individuals must take personal responsibility for the harm that they are deemed to cause others. Global solutions of the past have become local and personal hygiene problems for today.

Such is the circuitous logic and self-serving nature of contemporary public health campaigns that the World Health Organisation's Healthy Cities Network exists 'to strengthen the national standing of Healthy Cities'. ('I exist to promote my existence' sounds uncannily like Asimov's third Law of Robotics.) The World Health Organisation defines a Healthy City as

> a clean, safe physical environment of a high quality … an ecosystem that is stable now and sustainable in the long term; a strong mutually supportive and non-exploitative community … a diverse, vital and innovative economy … the encouragement of connectedness with the past, with the cultural and biological heritage of city dwellers and with other groups and individuals.

It is only after its vague wish-list of platitudes that the WHO deigns to mention the need for 'an optimum level of appropriate public health and sickness care services, accessible to all'.[10]

We may pretend that this shifting focus reflects the fact that real disease is less prevalent today than ever before; but it indicates a move away from healthcare as a practical, medical, physical reality and into the realm of 'lifestyle choices' and 'potential illness'. It invites the authorities to invade our private habits, individual autonomy and personal habits. This not only accepts unwarranted intrusions in our private lives, but also tends to absolve the authorities from any responsibility to maintain decent provision for genuine reasons of pubic health. In January 2011, when rats were filmed scurrying along the steps of 10 Downing Street, the subsequent media circus looked to an individual solution – also known as a cat – rather than raising any more generalised commentary about the remainder of central London's rat-infested streets.

Improving Versus Restricting Mobility

By the turn of the twentieth century in Britain, regulations to make order out of the chaos of bulging Victorian cities were beginning to encompass buildings, public health, highways, streets, and even whole cities. These rules were vital to the functioning of a city. They promised 'rights' to the public, such as clean water, energy on demand, clean air and the right to 'pass and repass on the Kings/Queen's highway' (as set out in the Highways Acts from 1835 to 1980). Authorities and legislation referred to streets and squares not as the 'public realm', but as the private domain of the Queen, who graciously allowed her subjects to use them. It has become familiar for such rights increasingly to be restrained by the sheer volume of traffic. Indeed, Albermarle Street, home to the Royal Institution, was the first designated one-way street in London, due to the physical impossibility of horse-drawn carriages passing each other along it.

The first thing to be said about congestion charging in London is that there were the same number of cars driving in central London in 2003 (just before the congestion charge was introduced) as there were in 1963 – which begs the question of whether it was such a problem as we were led to believe. It is also fair to say that congestion is one of the defining differences between a city and a village. After all, an uncongested city is, surely, a village.

Notwithstanding the fact that there is no clear definition of 'congestion', improving traffic flows through urban centres is a positive ambition. However, congestion charging achieves this by reducing the amount of people using the extant road network, rather than by increasing the supply. Introducing policies to stop people from driving is not the most progressive transport policy in the world. In fact, reducing the freedom of a mode of personal transport and hampering mobility is a contradictory element in Britain's so-called transport strategy.

Admittedly, road space has become increasingly constricted in urban areas, especially in London, but the rational solution is not to eke out a little bit more use from an ailing, finite road network; it is to provide more. In fact, road space in the UK generally has increased by only 25 per cent in the past 50 years, while the amount of traffic has increased by 700 per cent, so it is remarkable that the problem of congestion is not much worse than we now imagine it to be.

Parking meters were introduced in the late 1950s and 1960s to manage on-street parking in areas of high demand. They helped to ration and share the scarce resource of road space and, although a burden, their introduction was received with surprising equanimity by car-drivers. Compare this with the introduction of the London Congestion Charge, which was also formally introduced to ration scarce road space, but whose primary mechanism was one of apportioning blame, and we see that, in the latter case, driving became a moral – rather than a modal – choice.

Private Versus Public Drinking

Henry Ford used secret agents in the 1920s to invade his workers' houses, in order to ensure that they were not drinking at home. Such an intrusion used to be seen as reprehensible and authoritarian, but at least he had a direct employer–employee contractual interest in ensuring that his workers had the productive capacity of sobriety. Not so today, where individuals' drinking habits are now the business, it seems, of all sorts of officious strangers. The Licensing Act 2003 was a different animal altogether. It was concerned neither with the practical requirements of industry, nor with the need to ensure the safety of the alcohol being consumed. Instead, it explicitly, and for the first time, brought together controls over public behaviour concerning disorder, alcohol consumption, entertainment, planning, the environment, public health and public security. The fact that Mayor Boris Johnson's first 'transport' policy was to ban alcohol on the London Underground – a problem that many Londoners had not realised was a problem until that point – indicates that public health and security are often concepts imposed from the top down.

Smog Versus Smoke

While many institutions and networks were re-established after the Second World War, the relationship with central government had altered. Many of the post-war reforms, such as those regarding health, housing and planning, helped to foster perceptions of benign paternalism. But practical and progressive regulations were also introduced in the post-war period. A series of thick, acrid 'smogs' in the early 1950s (mixtures of smoke and fog in cities, which reduced visibility to less than one metre) resulted in parliament passing the Clean Air Act in 1956, which made most urban areas zones where only smokeless fuel could be burned. In London in 1952, a 'pea-souper' claimed the lives of 12,000 people,[11] so the legislation was brought in with health- and life-saving intentions. The fact that this problem of air pollution affected everyone required a broad-based solution. Ulrich Beck, Professor of Sociology at the London School of Economics, has pointed out that '[p]overty is hierarchic, smog is democratic'. Undoubtedly, wealthy homeowners could shut out the problem more easily than most. After all, the Great Stink of 1858 had been kept from the noses of many well-to-do MPs by the perfuming of the heavy curtains in parliament; a remedy not available to the poor.

Admittedly, in 1909, when 1,000 Glaswegians died in smog, a campaigner from the National Smoke Abatement Society at the time said that 'the deaths are the result of the actions of the citizens themselves', but ultimately that was simply a description rather than an indictment of individual behaviour and an injunction that Glaswegians should stop lighting fires, given that they had no real option when it came to keeping warm.

The example of these eminently sensible anti-smog campaigns is now held up as a model for anti-smoking campaigns. Two-thirds of the UK population does not smoke, and yet a seminal study states that 51 per cent of children in the UK are 'regularly exposed to second-hand smoke'.

This WHO report – written by its 'Tobacco-Free Initiative' – is loaded with such rhetorical, non-medical phrases (the 'tobacco epidemic',[12] for example), and argues that passive smoking (that is, inhaling the smoke of others), results in 600,000 deaths every year worldwide. Admittedly, the authors concede that 'to identify national data for second-hand smoke, the keywords "second hand smoke", "environmental tobacco smoke", and "passive smoking" were combined with names of countries or regions, by searching Google'.

Even if they did thoroughly assess the data, their conclusions assume that correlations are the same as causality. But it is the conclusions that interest us here. Unsurprisingly, the authors 'recommend that the provisions of the WHO Framework Convention on Tobacco Control should be enforced immediately to create complete smoke-free environments in all indoor workplaces, public places, and on public transport'. Regardless of the evidence (which is weak), science should not be used as an evidence-based policy tool to restrict the actions of citizens. As the political commentator Tim Black puts it, 'expertise should not be prostituted to politicians and political campaigners'.[13] Meanwhile, the Royal Society of Physicians insists that '[a]dults need to think about who's seeing them smoke' – to which the reply might be, mind your own business. Stick to public health.

The difference between then and now is clear. In the first instance, the dangers to health of the impenetrable smogs of the 1950s were well established. Secondly, the fact that domestic coal fires were one of the main causes of air pollution did not give rise to a crusade against coal users' influence on children's morals. Thirdly, the autonomy of the individual resided in the fact that better, cleaner fuels – or central-heating technologies emerging at the time – were available to ensure that people were able to enjoy high standards of home comfort.

The reverse of all these three conditions pertains today, where the process tends to follow the pattern: paranoid data, pointing the finger at blameworthy behaviour, leading to condemnations of unethical practices, resulting in demands for restrictive legislation and an injunction to self-restraint. This might be the kind of attitude beloved of small-town parochialists, but it now seems to be the position of choice for most metropolitan authorities.

The growing number of regulations and laws governing public behaviour in cities include many that require us to defer to higher authorities. That may be reasonable; but, in fact, CCTV spy cameras notwithstanding, British cities are not like East Germany circa 1984. Indeed, the instruments of the state are often absent. The key point is that we, the public, are not governed by a fear of the state, but increasingly by a fear of ourselves. When Margaret Thatcher talked of the 'enemy within', she was, at least, pointing to a real, conscious threat to state authority. When David Cameron uses similar rhetoric (demanding 'a commitment to society'[14]), he is simply aggrieved by louche behaviour.

With the dearth of true 'grittiness' on the streets, some commentators have feted the emergence of experimental city street 'drama'. Andy Beckett, writing in the *Guardian*, looks favourably on the 'guerrilla gardening movement and the boom in music festivals … the vogue for temporary "pop-up" shops, restaurants and cinemas in empty urban spaces'.[15] These events, of course, are not proliferating to the extent imagined by London journalists, even though they are a welcome addition to the tapestry of urban life. However, it is wishful thinking to assume that they are somehow transformative. Such over-flattery of random events was expounded by Stephen Duncombe in his book *Dream: Re-imagining Progressive Politics in an Age of Fantasy*.

Duncombe, a New York University academic and cycling activist with Reclaim the Streets, believes that we need to create myths and ambitious dreams in order to help motivate people to create a better future. 'Fantasy and spectacle', he says, 'have become the lingua franca of our time'.[16] However, his book carries with it the dangerous authoritarianism of the righteously like-minded: those who do not have to explain their rationale in political terms, but simply need to incite people to get on board. Ironically, a common assumption held by people taking part in these so-called 'countercultural' activities is that they are promulgating the 'correct', 'responsible' message without ever having to legitimise their views in the court of public opinion. We would go so far to say that self-appointed groups such as these are fundamentally undemocratic in believing that they have right on their side. Theirs is a version of Sixties Yippee radicalism without the politics.

Guerrilla gardening, for example, is about as radical as having someone break into your house while you are out – in order to redecorate and rearrange the furniture. Gangs of youths go out in the dead of night to plant shrubs in verges or cut the grass on roundabouts. With teenage rebellion like this, who needs local authority highway maintenance teams? It makes one long for antisocial behaviour to restore one's faith in the next generation. Pop-up restaurants are what restaurant critic A. A. Gill has called 'Pimpernel counter-chic'[17] – admirably proletarian but fundamentally bourgeois, and completely mainstream. Flash mobs – that other expression of political spontaneity – which are regularly non-political and never spontaneous, make a point of celebrating their mass individualism, rather than their collective consciousness.

These are sanitised versions of protest. They are safe and non-threatening and can be indulged in by the culturati. No one has been arrested; no one has been accused of irresponsibility. Indeed, the buzzword is 'fun'. David Tracey, the designated original guerrilla gardener says that '[t]he concept is simple, whimsical and has cheeky appeal'. The new face of fun protest is Banksy – he is urban, cool and wealthy; but if you are a disgruntled teenager with a spray-can and some attitude, you will still get nicked. There is, it seems, graffiti and then there is respectable graffiti (or 'art'). Even *Top Gear* (the car programme for petrolheads), which was criticised by a select committee for suggesting that 'there is virtue in driving too quickly',[18] toned down and agreed to be more responsible. It now keeps to the speed limit on main roads and does the 'fun stuff' off-road.

AUTONOMY

From as far back as Thomas Hobbes, there has been an understandable desire to impose social order: 'For the differences of private men, to declare what is equity, what is justice, and is moral virtue, and to make them binding, there is need of the ordinances of sovereign power, and punishments to be ordained for such as shall break them.'[19] But a great liberal commentator, J. S. Mill remarked:

> the only purpose for which power can be rightfully exercised over any member of a civilized community, against his will, is to prevent harm to others. His own good, either physical or moral, is not a sufficient warrant … Over himself, over his own body and mind, the individual is sovereign.[20]

Public space should be where individuals see, and are seen by, others as they engage in public affairs. It is the space for civic and cultural interaction. In her book *On Revolution*, Hannah Arendt, the twentieth-century political philosopher, links this space with the 'public freedom' generated by our free activity, which, in turn, requires the space within which to exercise that freedom.

Unfortunately, to some degree, today's urban life and civic development are ever more bounded by rules and regulations that undermine that interpersonal trust. All new developments in UK cities now have to meet a series of security requirements. They have to ensure 'secure by design', 'defensible space', 'liveable spaces' and 'walkable environments', each with implicit and explicit messages to ensure 24-hour monitoring. Jane Jacobs's 1961 classic, *The Death and Life of Great American Cities*, argued that real safety in the city comes from 'natural surveillance' by strangers with their eyes on the street. But, for this to work, the logical prerequisite is the independent existence of a feeling of trust among strangers. She observed that 'its cultivation cannot be institutionalized' by the authorities.

Of late, we know what is expected of us – namely, to behave 'responsibly' – and we moderate our actions accordingly. It has become natural to frown on unacceptably 'irresponsible' behaviour, which is not to say that we are more intolerant: mercifully, we no longer look down our noses at gays or black people; neither do we pillory single parents, or express exasperation at adulterers. However, light up a cigarette, drive an SUV, pester people with a leaflet, take a photograph of a public building, or behave in a way that might be perceived by others as intimidating, and you will understand that there is still a great deal of behaviour that is unacceptable. Formerly innocent behaviour is treated, for no good reason, with suspicion. Ironically, the very people who protested against the earlier expressions of intolerance are all too often the same people who are intolerant of contemporary behaviour.

Indeed, we have internalised the reason why intrusive regulations and monitoring devices were introduced in the first place: the sense that the *potential* for deviant behaviour lurks everywhere. We have accepted that other people are potentially harmful rather than helpful, and thus the notion of the 'public' has broken down somewhat.

We are increasingly encouraged – in a sense, obliged – to snoop, as voyeurs of private actions. This is where the breakdown in trust is sharpest. Here the attack on self takes on a more severe character, for the private sphere is where we should be most independent and autonomous, sharing with a small number of known individuals, rather than exposed to a wider public. This is where we need intimacy, support and tolerance. Instead we get suspicion. We are encouraged to be voyeurs – checking on each other, and checking up on each other. The official endorsement of whistle-blowing is the logical extension of that distrustful syndrome.

Transparency and knowledge of each other is the new openness; but there are some things best kept to oneself, some activities best done in private, individually, or with others in a safe, intimate environment. Sociologist Frank Furedi has noted that

> transparency is upheld because people are not trusted to do the right thing unless they are held to account by rules, procedures and, of course, a paper trail. It is a convergence of uncertainty about the capacity to know and mistrust of human behaviour which fuels the conspiratorial imagination and the deification of transparency.[21]

The *cri de cœur* of reasonable citizens everywhere is: 'If you've done nothing wrong, you've nothing to hide'. This eminently logical sentiment has legitimised the intervention into the private sphere for many years; but nowadays the flipside assumption is that if you are hiding something, you have done something wrong. Gone is the comfort of having secrets. Admittedly, the state is not heavy-handedly insisting that we show our papers and reveal where we are going – but it is a cultural pressure that pressurises us to 'admit' things ourselves. The corrosive aspect of such self-doubt (the tacit internalising of a broad social suspicion of others) leaves us helpless. Writer and activist Josie Appleton reviewed *Privacy: A Manifesto*, by the German sociologist Wolfgang Sofsky, concluding:

The 'transparent' citizen has nothing to hide, maybe, but nothing can be created, nothing resisted and so conformity in a sanitized environment is all that is left. We watch and are watched, voyeur and exhibitionist – flat, sterile and totally lacking imagination and character.[22]

It is ironic that this situation is portrayed by many as an open public engagement, when in fact it is corrosive of the very informalities that give the public sphere its frisson. As a result, in many instances, gone is the 'edginess' of the city, and in its place has emerged a sanitised version – cleansed of conflict, argument, debate, protest, intimacy, informality, noise. We may witness these occasionally – and be shocked by them precisely because of their rarity – but the sense of these potential rifts, ructions and ribaldry within civic space being prevalent fizzled out long ago. Once hailed as the defining characteristic of a vibrant public life, discord is far too disruptive for a safe city. Rather than officialdom's iron fist, it is the censorious velvet glove of self-regulation that dampens social engagement today.

Learning to trust each other in neighbourhoods could help build social tolerance and active understanding. If localism and the 'Big Society' enable this, then they could go some way to restoring notions of public freedom. The constraint on this happening is the explicit parochialism that underpins them. If individuals can trust people only within their own neighbourhood, then there is very limited opportunity to be tolerant of more than a minority of society. More worryingly, those people within urban neighbourhoods who want to assert their private right *not* to be part of a Big Society street party, or a community activity programme, or a fun run, will find themselves asked why, and quietly ostracised. The right to refuse community participation is as fundamental as the desire to achieve it. In Mill's phrase, 'the individual is sovereign'.

NOTES

1. William H. Whyte, 'The Social Life of Small Urban Spaces', Municipal Art Society of New York, 1980.

2. Corinna Ferguson, 'Do the Police Have the Power to Break Up Groups of Innocent Friends?' *Guardian*, 19 March 2010, at <www.guardian.co.uk/commentisfree/libertycentral/2010/mar/19/police-power-disperse-small-groups>.

3. BBC News, 'Purple Flag Awards for Six "Safe" Town Centres', 4 November 2008, at <www.bbc.co.uk/news/uk-england-11691803>.

4. Joanna Sugden, 'Most Violent Places to Live in England', *Times*, 22 August 2008.

5. Quoted in P. D. Smith, 'Woolworth's Shrine to Commerce: The Limitless Ambitions, and Problematic Achievements, of Science and Urban Planning in the Early Twentieth Century', *Times Literary Supplement*, 28 January 2009.

6. Ed Hollis, 'Be Careful What You Wish For, Dave', *Building Design*, 18 February 2011, p. 9.

7. BBC News online, 'What Every Brit Should Know about Jaywalking', 12 January 2007, at <news.bbc.co.uk/1/hi/6251431.stm>.

8. Channel 4 News website, 'Factcheck: How Many CCTV Cameras?', 18 June 2008.

9. Ibid.

10. World Health Organisation, 'Urban Health: Healthy City Checklist', at <www.euro.who.int/en/what-we-do/health-topics/environmental-health/urban-health/activities/healthy-cities/who-european-healthy-cities-network/what-is-a-healthy-city/healthy-city-checklist>.

11. Michelle L. Bell and Devra Lee Davis, 'Reassessment of the Lethal London Fog of 1952: Novel Indicators of Acute and Chronic Consequences of Acute Exposure to Air Pollution', *Environmental Health Perspectives* 109, supplement 3 (June 2001).

12. Mattias Öberg, Maritta S. Jaakkola, Alistair Woodward, Armando Peruga and Annette Prüss-Ustün, 'Worldwide Burden of Disease from Exposure to Second-Hand Smoke: A Retrospective Analysis of Data from 192 Countries', *Lancet*, 26 November 2010, p. 6.

13. Tim Black, 'The New Priesthood of Meddling Experts', *Spiked*, 25 March 2010, at <www.spiked-online.com/index.php/site/article/8343>.

14. David Cameron, 'Let's Mend Our Broken Society', speech at the Conservative Party Conference, 27 April 2010.

15. Andy Beckett, 'The New Public Space: How Britons Have Reclaimed the Streets', *Guardian*, 20 August 2010.

16. Stephen Duncombe, 'Dream: Re-Imagining Progressive Politics in an Age of Fantasy', *New Press*, 2006.

17. A. A. Gill, 'Casa Brindisa', *Sunday Times*, 22 February 2009.

18. Select Committee on Environment, Transport and Regional Affairs, 'Inquiry into Young and Newly-Qualified Drivers: Standards and Training', ETRA, 2009.

19. Thomas Hobbes, *Leviathan*, Penguin Classics, 1982, p. 185.

20. J. S. Mill, *On Liberty*, Oxford Paperbacks, 1998, p. 9.

21. Frank Furedi, 'Frank Furedi on the Cult of Leaking', *Spiked*, at <www.spiked-online.com/index.php/essays/article/10270>, 9 March 2011.

22. Josie Appleton, 'Why Privacy Matters: Surveillance and Regulation are Harming Our Humanity', *Spiked Review of Books*, July 2010.

7
The Eco-City
Utopia, Then and Now

Austin Williams

I have never felt salvation in nature. I love cities above all.
Michelangelo Antonioni, *Life Magazine*

Ecological urbanist Richard Register is said to have coined the term 'eco-cities' to describe a 'non-violent city' – a place in which to 'make peace on Earth and with Earth'.[1] Environmental academic Rodney White says that it is 'a city that provides an acceptable standard of living for its human occupants without depleting the ecosystems and biochemical cycles on which it depends'.[2] The *Financial Times* is a little less woolly, outlining the key requirements of an eco-city to be

> a self-contained economy; 100 per cent carbon-neutral energy production; an interconnected transport system and land-use pattern that shifts people from cars to walking, cycling and public transport; a zero-waste management system; resource conservation, including maximising water and energy efficiency and preserving open land, wildlife and plant habitats; and using environmentally sound building materials, preferably locally sourced.[3]

What all these definitions have in common is the notion that an eco-city is one concerned with its environmental impacts; those that a 'normal', or what is sometimes called an 'instant' city is assumed to flout. First of all, to assess the claims of environmental benefit, I will use typical sustainability criteria to compare a new state-of-the-art eco-city with a 'normal' city. Let us compare Tianjin in China, which is due for completion in 2020, with London today. I will use the eco-criteria set out in Tianjin's own press statements as the basis of the comparison.

Public transport is central to Tianjin's project, and it is expected that 90 per cent of urban journeys will be by means other than the private car. Surprisingly, maybe, this is exactly the same percentage of public transport trips taken by those who currently commute into central London.[4] In terms of carbon emissions, London's are currently nearly half of those projected for Tianjin, at just 99 tons per US$1 million of GDP, compared to Tianjin's 150 tons. Admittedly, these figures may be hostage to economic performance, which is perhaps why Tianjin chooses this benchmark.

Since October 2011, all new domestic developments in London have a notional maximum water-consumption rate of 120 litres per person per day, as set out in the Building Regulations. This, too, is the same as Tianjin aims for in ten years' time. Finally, London has 105 sqare metres of green space per person – almost nine times that proposed for purpose-built Tianjin. On a like-for-like basis, it would seem that London is actually way ahead – in environmental terms – of a purpose-built Chinese eco-city.

Undoubtedly, on a number of other indicators London compares less favourably. For example, the UK's Renewable Energy Strategy aims for 15 per cent of all energy to be produced from renewable sources by 2020 (and London is currently well below that target), compared to Tianjin's 20 per cent. Furthermore, because of its old stock, one third of London's homes – including Buckingham Palace[5] – have leaky single-glazed windows and inadequate insulation, whereas *all* of Tianjin's 120,000 new dwellings will be insulated and double-glazed. However, because of the size of London, even at today's low build rates, there are already three times as many homes in London built to a comparable standard. Meanwhile, just 25 per cent of London's waste is recycled (most of London's rubbish is incinerated), compared to Tianjin's 60 per cent.

While some of these indicators of London's environmental performance are below those of the Tianjin eco-city it is in any case worth questioning the merit of many of these indicators. For instance, it could be argued that high water use is a symbol of better standards of living (the fact that Mozambicans typically use just five litres of water per person per day is nothing to be admired). Similarly, there is little inherently positive about recycling. Even though the United Nations boasts that 'about 1–2 percent of the world's urban population sustain their livelihood by collecting and recycling paper, cardboard, plastic, and metal waste',[6] perhaps that reality should be seen as a source of shame. At the start of the global recession, when the price of rubbish collapsed, many UK local authorities and recycling storage facilities finally realised that they were simply stockpiling garbage: neither healthy nor admirable. They were merely 'fuelling the 80 million strong rat population'.[7]

If the gains are not so clear-cut, is there anything positive about the eco-city label? Why is it uncritically accepted as the new way forward? This chapter will explore the rationale, rather than the statistical justification, for eco-cities, and will examine whether they should be hailed as exemplars of a new way of urban living. It will focus predominantly on China – the country that proposed the world's first eco-city in Dongtan. Research suggests that there are already a further 160 eco-cities in development.[8]

PREFIX-CITIES

Across the world, cities are latching on to the label. Freiburg has rebranded itself from Germany's 'solar city' to its 'eco-city'; Zaragoza in Spain now markets its eco-city status on the back of its 'bioclimatic housing units' (these are buildings that minimise their reliance on mechanical conditioning); and the Hacienda in Mombasa pledges to use 'minimal natural resources'.[9] Such is the lure of the prefix that relatively inconsequential villages are re-badging themselves as eco-cities. Often, too, their claims to environmental status are not particularly appealing: India's Manesar will become its first eco-city based on recycling industrial waste, and Johannesburg's eco-city is situated in a township (where, says the United Nations, the 'concept of "sweat equity" is regularly utilized'[10]). Meanwhile, Libya's eco-city has stalled, Dongtan has failed, Addis Ababa never really took off, and Huangbaiyu has ended in bitter recriminations.

Researcher Shannon May has been rigorous in her documentation of the environmental failings at Huangbaiyu, a small village south-east of Shenyang in the north-eastern Liaoning province of China. In the obsequious media coverage that followed its launch, it is described as an eco-city, but it is actually a small rural area undergoing a trial development. It comprises just 400 dwellings. The hype did not stop there; there is seldom any meaningful critical analysis of developments with an 'eco' prefix, unless and until they fall apart. Even then, it is shameful how quickly such failures are hushed up.

Initiated by Bill McDonough, the so-called 'Green Dean' of the University of Virginia and author of the 'cradle-to-cradle' concept of holistic environmental planning, Huangbaiyu was hailed as one of the early interventions in China's urban environmental revolution. In fact, it is now alleged that, instead of being a triumph of environmental engineering, the China-US Centre for Sustainable Development (a company that McDonough formed with Deng Xioping's daughter) took more than five years to construct just 40 eco-houses. Worse, these are properties that no one either seems to want or can afford.[11]

May was an anthropologist in the village at the time of McDonough's intervention, and is scathing about his involvement. Her essay 'Ecological Modernism and the Making of a New Working Class'[12] examines the raised hopes and unrealistic environmental mandates, as well as the consequent economic hardship, caused to the locals in this 'model' proposal. It seems that the villagers were convinced that they should demolish their existing dwellings and build replacement eco-homes on the understanding that major investment would follow. Allegedly, they agreed on the basis that the housing was a mere precursor to industrial development and employment opportunities, replicating a little bit of what they knew was happening in the rest of China. It appears that they were convinced by the fact that an American was backing the scheme assuming that it would be a lucrative success and a business worth supporting.

Not only was that a forlorn hope, but the eco-demands imposed on the villagers caused genuine distress. No industry was planned or ever really intended; agricultural land was taken from them to develop the scheme, leaving them with backyard 'subsistence gardens';[13] biomass heating systems relied on burning the corn husks that were the staple diet of their livestock; the roofs leaked; the solar investment failed to materialise; and the green construction techniques resulted in houses that would eventually cost ten times a villagers' median income. Green pioneer Rob Watson, who has helped the Chinese Ministry of Construction develop its sustainable building standards, says that 'the whole experiment was touted as a success long after it failed. Nobody's living there, nobody moved in. It's sitting there, literally, rotting.'[14] Regardless of the collapse of the concept, Huangbaiyu is still regularly feted in the environmental press as a worthy experiment or a work in progress. While Western blame is often casually apportioned to the Chinese contractor and the local bureaucracy, it is clear that the concept was flawed from the start.

Without meaningful development (which means economic and industrial progress as opposed to just urban design), villagers are condemned to continue their lives of agricultural hardship. Perhaps this is hardly surprising, given that the logic – and the essence – of the eco-city ideology is critical of rapid material improvement, eco-advocates often arguing that it runs counter to the wishes of the people and, more importantly, to the 'carrying capacity' of the local environment. Huangbaiyu, after all, was an eco-demonstration project – a way of enhancing people's ecologically sensitive lifestyle by reducing their impact, minimising their footprint and reducing their consumption models; in other words, an instance of peasant agriculture. Ironically, the more that indigenous working practices were maintained, the better the zero-carbon results, and the more the project's supporters could justify its existence.

FEWER CHOICES

As we have seen from the definitions of eco-cities at the start of the chapter, the concept tends to portray the city as an *organism* (a microcosm of James Lovelock's Gaia hypothesis, which sees the earth as 'behaving as if it were alive'[15]). This proposition is a rhetorical device to describe the harms that carbon-centric urban agglomerations produce, and the benefits that sustainable urbanity can bring. However, this conceptualisation of human habitation is premised on the misanthropic assumption that such a human-, rather than nature-centric desire is a problem that has to be reined in. In order to minimise our impact, environmentalists agree, we have to reduce our selfish ambitions to consume more. Under this characterisation, clearly subsistence is the most sustainable path.

Admittedly, this ruralist logic is seldom explicit, and the modern framework of developmental urbanisation disguises its ratiocination; but it is clear that many advocates of eco-cities prefer a labour-intensive existence to a resource-intensive life-style. Unfortunately, many environmentalists indeed conclude that people should reduce their materialist aspirations in order to protect nature, rather than nature being at man's disposal to improve his or her social and material ambitions. Shannon May notes that the eco-city logic means that the lives and means of survival of rural residents of Huangbaiyu were seen as 'just their equivalence in carbon'. She points out that this type of green deal ends up with 'programs to save the planet from the peril of industrialization [that] do so on the broken backs of the rural poor all over the world'.[16]

The battle between freedom and restraint has a long history in the western canon (and indeed in the global canon, if there were such a thing[17]), and throughout a large part of the twentieth century it has manifested itself in a defence of western liberal values against illiberalism. Of late, the framework of sustainability has blurred the distinction, as the environmental hegemony seeks to subvert individual autonomy and encroach on the minutiae of life. As Green Alliance activist Julie Hill writes of western consumers: 'we actually need ... to have some choices taken away from us'.[18] The frustration of environmentalists at the awakened materialism of Chinese villagers, who, as they claim, are 'making the same mistake as us', regularly takes on an acrimonious form. One writer says 'China's top-down, authoritarian development model – an unyielding machine greatly more efficient than that of messy democracy – could apply to ecological as well as economic progress ... if China wills it, it has the power to impose environmentalism by fiat'.[19]

All too often, western environmental commentators rail against the non-renewable, energy-driven growth of the Chinese economy, criticising the Communist elite's single-minded capitalist expansion, but they are paradoxically enamoured by the power of the one-party state to nudge people's changes in behaviour using the same authoritarian power structure. As far as many of them are concerned, growth is harmful (bad), whereas restraint is morally good; and thus the mechanisms to impose, enforce or encourage limits become acceptable if they are shown to be environmentally effective. James Brearly, urbanist and adjunct professor at the Royal Melbourne Institute of Technology, notes that '[t]he so-called democratic nations are impotent when it comes to making urgent necessary changes. China can change systems that will serve the good and aren't depending on the will of the people or business to be altruistic.'[20]

While arch-environmentalist Fred Pearce longs for 'the emergence of an older, more mature, less frenetic, less consumerist, and more frugal society',[21] I think that we need to be watchful of the austere and anti-democratic logic of eco-cities. To do this, we need to open our eyes to what is actually going on in the name of environmental urbanism and be more critical of its objectives, not just its effects. Unfortunately, in many instances, commentators are blind to the problematic realities of eco-city development.

UNDERDEVELOPED PLANS

Dongtan was the most high-profile eco-city of the first decade of the twenty-first century: the first serious attempt to engineer environmental criteria into urban planning in China. Alex Steffen, the ex-editor of WorldChanging.com, who describes himself as a 'planetary futurist', could not stress the importance of this project enough, saying that 'on projects like Dongtan hinge the fate of our planet'.[22] He was not alone. Very many commentators threw caution to the wind in their paean to Dongtan's imminent world-saving potential.

Situated on Chongming Island, near Shanghai (one of the locations of Mao's forced-labour 're-education' centres during the Cultural Revolution), it was master-planned by the international engineering company Arup in 2003. The Anglo-Chinese project was pushed through by Tony Blair and Hu Jintao in 2005, and the 80,000-dwelling urban centre was scheduled for completion in time for the Shanghai Expo in 2010.

By 2009 it was becoming increasingly clear that Dongtan had failed to materialise. The site had been cleared, the farmers and peasants moved off the land, and large areas prepared, but, as one observer put it, 'no construction has occurred there – indeed it's gone backwards, as a visitor centre previously built is now shut'.[23] All references to it were quickly airbrushed from both the Shanghai Expo's and Arup's websites.

The fact that one of the lead backers of the project, former Communist Party chief Chen Liangyu, was sentenced to 18 years in prison for bribery and abuse of power in 2008 cannot have helped. Similarly, there were undoubtedly problems concerning the use of challenging technologies, lapsed planning permissions, and the alleged greed of major international consultancies that were riding in on the Chinese eco-urban gold-rush. But why did no-one spot that the project was floundering? The simple fact is that nobody ever questioned the hype; everyone was enjoying the hype too much. Computer-generated bird's-eye images of generic eco-city proposals featured in architectural magazines across the world, and Arup found itself the centre of an eco-renaissance of global urban sustainability. But 'sustainable development' is not the same as 'development': it is, in fact, a symbol of the philosophical rejection of the positive connotations of development itself. Sustainable development embodies the hope that the developing world will slow down (fortuitously, to the competitive advantage of ailing Western economies).

A decade ago, a Japanese writer described how, historically, 'the West represents Modernity, and Asia must, ipso facto represent Countermodernity'.[24] When this was written, it was intended to be a description of the backward nature of the East as opposed to the West. Today, that same sentence might just as well represent a commentary on the profligate nature of the modern West and the clamour for an 'alternative model of development'.[25] Today's anti-progressive, low-growth sentiments must be avoided if the poor are to be able to continue to climb quickly out of poverty, but also so that national economies can improve. The fact that, after years of repression, the Chinese people are now grasping with both hands the opportunity presented by material growth is hardly surprising.

By 1956, practically all of the farming households in China were coerced into cooperatives. These units merged 40 to 100 villages in communes to labour for what was called the 'common good'.[26] During the period from 1968 to 1978, official Chinese policy was systematically to de-urbanise or 'ruralise' the urban population. Sixteen million urban students were sent to become farmers, for example. This social necessity, as it was described, was due to the lack of dynamic in the industrial sectors, and yet even this enforced migration did not hide rising unemployment figures.[27] There was nothing natural or desirable about Chinese farming; in fact, the recent economic revolution has been predicated on ever-decreasing levels of employment in the agricultural sector, as people abandon the land for a better chance in life.

The repressive regime of forced agricultural labour turned a blind eye to the maintenance by individuals of 'private plots',[28] in order that the peasantry might subsidise their meagre food intake and increase their own personal consumption levels. Today, even though the Five-Year Plan (2011–15) advocates 'consumption-led growth' as the way forward, the eco-cities mantra tends to be 'low consumption, low growth'. Whatever the diktat from on high, under the rubric of sustainability, eco-city residents have a personal responsibility not to exceed their environmentally-determined consumption parameters. But the fact that eco-city proposals include urban farms and actively promote opportunities for residents to grow their own local produce, the absorption of the rural experience into the urban context is complete. *Plus ça change.*

The new eco-city at Wanzhuang will absorb 40,000 agricultural workers and a number of existing villages into its growth plan. Engineering firm Arup is steering Wanzhuang's sustainable future to 'preserve, harness and enhance the established local traditions and agricultural knowledge'.[29] As the house magazine of the Royal Institute of British Architects explains, 'local farmers will be given the choice of staying in their own village or relocating to either a new urban area or a rural farmers' collective, which will adopt ecologically-based agricultural production to provide a local food supply, increase soil fertility and minimise pollution'.[30] It promises to have a minimal carbon footprint precisely because 'traditional' peasant agriculture, bicycle transport and wildlife habitats will be prioritised. In other words, Wanzhuang eco-city, is effectively a collective farm!

Such a blinkered approach inspired architect Bill McDonough to conceptualise an urban plan for Liuzhou in China that minimises its disturbance of the agricultural land on which it sits by lifting the original ground-level paddy fields onto the roof. In this instance, biodiversity becomes sacrosanct, while back-breaking rice production is relocated several floors up. What McDonough seems to have been oblivious to is that most Chinese peasants want to escape the paddies, not to have them elevated to new heights of importance.

In the eco-city rewriting of history, we in the West, it seems, have had it tough. We have had to endure car journeys from suburban semis to supermarkets stocked with global produce, in which we have been stressed by the choices available to us. Conversely, as the *New Statesman* romantically reported, Dongtan eco-city is where 'car dependence' will be avoided, and 'healthy food' will be produced 'by local farmers and fishermen' to 'ensure a healthy lifestyle' and 'create inclusive, cohesive and tolerant communities'.[31] While this smacks, not of architecture, but of social-policy diktat (of the type described in Chapter 6), the striking thing is that many commentators chose to ignore the intrusive nature of this eco-version of the *Little Red Book*. As the flattery was heaped on Dongtan, it seems as if hardly any questions were raised – even by architects – about the layout, the design, or even the quality of the architecture. That is just as well, because the project was seldom revealed; we were treated only to ubiquitous aerial computer images containing little or no detail. Certainly, hardly anyone raised the alarm as it became increasingly apparent that Dongtan was just not happening. Presumably, this was because everyone was in denial that the materialist China that the designers were attempting to subvert (or ignore) was actually appealing to real Chinese people – not those represented in computer models – who had a desire for speed, efficiency, personal mobility and industrialised, globalised food stocks: in other words, for *more* choices, not fewer. Environmentalists were all too busy promoting the low-growth, zero-impact, carbon-neutral, pedal-powered, eco-centric cliché, and failed to notice that things had moved on.

There is a growing literature suggesting that these eco-cities failed as a consequence of being too ambitious. Tragically, the opposite is true. China is a rapidly developing country with massive areas of underdevelopment. In order to raise such regions out of penury, improve housing and increase productive employment, development needs to be immediate, swift and, in many areas emphatically carbon-intensive. Dongtan was nowhere near ambitious enough.

DON'T MENTION THE INDUSTRY

For every failed project, there is another waiting to prove itself. As one scheme dies, so another emerges to take its place, and currently China is bursting with eco-cities. As we have seen, there are currently 160 eco-cities on the drawing board, up from 40 at the start of 2009: from Rizhao, in Shangdon province (a 'solar-powered city' of 3 million people[32]), to GuangMing, in the north-west of Shenzhen ('a smart city ... driven by the principles of slow living'[33]); from Wanzhuang, near Beijing ('bridging the urban–rural gap'[34]), to Caofeidian eco-city, near Tangshan (a 'model city of Fashion, Innovation, Green and Happiness'.[35] One Chinese author says that there is 'a fever of eco-city in China'.[36]

So have the lessons been learned, and is the grass now really greener in an eco-city? What type of life is proposed in these next-generation, low-carbon paradises, built in some of the most heavily industrialising regions of the world? Let us take a look at a few of the high-profile new players.

Caofeidian eco-city, a carbon-neutral city for 400,000 inhabitants, is a classic case study. Scheduled for completion in 2020, it is located in the Tangshan region of eastern China. This coastal area suffered a devastating earthquake in 1976 that killed 270,000 people, and since then the *China Daily* states that it has undergone '10 years of reconstruction, 10 years revitalisation and another 10 years of new development'.[37] In fact, Caofeidian is now a major industrial and bulk-shipping port. It has a gigantic oil refinery and handles vast coal shipments, making it northern China's second-biggest coal port to Qinhuangdao.

Because pollution levels could not be addressed by retrofitting its original plant, the Capital Steel and Iron Corporation transferred its entire operation from Shijiangshan, near Beijing, to Caofeidian's new reclamation site on the coast. Many of its 10,000 workers have had to move 220 kilometres to keep their jobs. As the industrial port grows, so a residential city has had to grow up to house the workers and to meet their needs and aspirations. Notwithstanding the four 250,000-ton mineral terminals, two 300,000-ton crude oil terminals, sixteen 50,000–100,000 ton coal terminals, and one 100,000-ton liquefied natural gas terminal,[38] it is the workers' city that has attracted the eco-label.

This is not intended to be a finger-wagging exposé of Asia's urban greenwashing, but rather to set the city in context. It is commonplace for environmentalists to suggest that Chinese eco-cities are PR cloaks behind which hides the most polluted country on earth. Such criticism serves to condemn Chinese industrialisation that has, *inter alia*, lifted 300 million people out of poverty in the last decade, and has actually provided the context – financial and cultural – within which to realise the aspiration for a less polluted environment.

Caofeidian's urban agglomeration is similar in intent to Pearl Village in Qatar, Shell's Pearl gas-to-liquid plant dormitory city, which houses 40,000 workers and a staff of 1,800 from 70 countries. Unlike Caofeidian, Pearl Village prides itself on a vast network of air-conditioned dormitories, which are 10 minutes' drive from the construction site. While Shell is seldom believed when it states that such developments are 'in line with our sustainable development principles' (its processing plant, for example, 'will be the world's largest, recovering, treating and re-using all the industrial process water'[39]), many serious green commentators on Caofeidian choose to ignore the hard industrial and petrochemical reality behind its creation. But the fact is that it is the economic growth and speedy wealth-generation in China – from places like this – that has provided it with the luxury of developing decent eco-housing for its workers.

Similiarly, Masdar City, in Qatar, is held aloft as the new future for eco-city development, but it too is just a few miles away from the oil-fields of Abu Dhabi. I shall look briefly at Masdar later, but it seems that what inspires eco-urbanists to sing the praises of these foreign developments is that, to them, they are blank slates. If western oil money is involved, then the project is viewed cynically and deemed to be tainted; however, if the resources come from the developing world itself, then they are often held up as exemplars of how these simple, plucky civilisations are exploring alternative development paths. In fact, the money may still come from crude oil, but Asian investment in eco-cities signifies to some western activists that China is trying not to follow the crude western path of materialism. It is thus common for environmentalists to criticise Western progress as the route of all evil, and praise Asian orientalism – its otherness – for its innocent and ancient natural rhythms. A South Korean academic observes:

> Korea's aspirations for development have mirrored the life-styles and economic achievements of developed countries. Very recently, however, Korean people have begun to realize that these life-styles and economic achievements lead rapidly to environmental degradation. It is now perceived that developed countries are far away from sustainability as it is defined within Korean tradition.[40]

'Tradition', meaning something that is not tainted by modernity, is often a euphemism for a direct relationship with nature –

which, in turn is something of a hallmark of a peasant economy. It is also, as we have seen, a common justification for Chinese eco-city status.

In reality, ordinary Chinese cities (that is, those without the eco-prefix) have grown in wealth, with a concomitant rise in living standards. Shanghai, for example, is currently the 25th-richest metropolitan area by GDP in the world. However, an old Chinese proverb says, 'With money you can buy a house, but not a home', and accordingly, many are now turning their attention to the need for the quality to go with the quantity – in other words, there is a search for a more rounded and benign development. Notwithstanding the overarching 'central task' of the Chinese regime to grow the economy (and maintain a fairly rigid political framework within which to do it), the common phrase heard in much Chinese urbanism is the desire to construct a 'harmonious society', described as a mix of 'the humanistic quality, social progress, and ecological civilization'.[41]

These are eminently reasonable ambitions for those struggling with the growing levels of pollution in many urban and peri-urban areas, but why does this simple demand for a better quality of life attract the 'eco' label? Undoubtedly, China is flaunting its sustainability credentials to the rest of the world and cocking a snook at critics of its relentless development by insisting, 'growth is good but it must be green'.[42] More pragmatically, international environmental standards, like the ISO 14000 management frameworks, are forcing China to buy into eco-certification if they want to continue trading globally.[43] But beyond these technicalities, beloved of China, there is an ideological rationale for the preponderance of eco-cities, and its aetiology resides in the dissatisfaction within the West.

In June 2007, the British prime minister, Gordon Brown, announced a programme to build five eco-towns (note: not 'eco-cities'), amounting to 25,000 carbon-neutral homes, each situated on under-used land or old industrial sites. Brown used his Party conference in September 2007 to announce a further five locations, so that there would be 'at least one [eco-town] in each region'.[44] Admittedly, aiming to create a new 'home-owning, asset-owning, wealth-owning democracy'[45] just before the housing market crash was an unfortunate move; but it was thought that, by utilising old 'brownfield' sites and derelict Ministry of Defence land, the initiative would at least not provoke criticism. Unfortunately, by 2010 only four sites had been earmarked, and funding had been slashed. To a large extent, the British eco-towns experiment is as low-key and boring as befits a tired western political project dedicated to restraint. Gordon Brown's eco-towns have indeed succeeded in making no impact on the planet at all.

PROMETHEUS UNBOUND

This year, the Communist Party of China's '12th Five-Year Plan for National Economic and Social Development' aims, among other things, to build 'a fairer society ... raise minimum wages and basic pensions [and] reverse the trend of a widening income gap'.[46] Warm words and fine objectives, but these ambitions have to be realised in the political, economic and social arena; they cannot be addressed, in microcosm, by an appeal to adopt a way of life or a particular urban form.

The prospective eco-city of Tianjin boasts 'a living environment that fosters community spirit and social harmony ... transformed into a new retail, food and beverage and wellness destination ... a vibrant city which caters to the hopes of its residents and builds up desirable civic values'.[47] The rhetorical flourishes of eco-city promoters sound a lot like the utopian socialist experiments of yesteryear, where a few liberal Victorian industrialists set up discrete, ring-fenced industrial communities in order to provide a less exploitative quality of life. Just as then, contemporary eco-city utopias comprise pre-planned settlement layouts and reforming zeal, imagining a better world in isolated economies, communitarian organisation, localized populations, moral strictures to improve the lot of the inhabitants, and the hope that they will act as pioneers, encouraging others to follow. However, while modern eco-cities are driven by a misanthropic disdain for human profligacy, the utopian socialist experiments were driven by a humanistic revulsion at human immiseration.

Two hundred years ago, the brutal development of early Victorian cities, with their oppressive living and working conditions, led to a radicalisation of established opinion. The pollution, squalor and casual disregard for human life – especially on the part of the employing classes in the industrialised centres – caused many to rethink the direction, acceptability and legitimacy of the social relations of early capitalism. Engels, writing famously about mid-century Manchester, noted that,

> In the industrial epoch alone has it become possible that the worker scarcely freed from feudal servitude could be used as mere material, a mere chattel; that he must let himself be crowded into a dwelling too bad for every other, which he for his hard-earned wages buys the right to let go utterly to ruin.[48]

Historian Tristram Hunt explains that Engels was appalled but not politicised by these bleak observations. In fact it was the other way around, and these vignettes served to illustrate and illuminate his political critique. Hunt says that they provided 'the essential data to flesh out his pre-existing philosophy'.[49]

Engels's book *The Condition of the Working Class in England in 1844* was a tour de force. It was a graphic argument for the need for societal transformation to alleviate the iniquitous position of the industrial working class. Engels advocated a rejection of the social organisation that led to such exploitation. Tinkering with it, he observed, would merely soften the harsh edges of capitalist society; and in his own sphere of direct influence, as a Manchester industrialist himself, he knew that amelioration was not sufficiently transformative.

Engels's rejection of social reformism found fuller expression in his later critique of utopian socialism, but he did acknowledge a debt to its historically specific, groundbreaking work. Among those critical early utopians were intellectual luminaries such as Saint-Simon, who wished to create order by the furtherance of industry and science; Fourier, who lauded the progressive power of reason; and Robert Owen, who, simply by placing his workers in 'conditions worthy of human beings', created a socially stable and harmonious colony of workers. While all of them have their resonances today, Owen's New Lanark seems to be an early physical expression of a socially sustainable human settlement.

Now a World Heritage Site, New Lanark was the home to Owen's heroic social experiment during the Industrial Revolution. Effective from the turn of the nineteenth century, the town comprised Owen's own house, his industrial premises, his workers' residences, schools and public buildings set alongside the River Clyde, which in turn powered the textile mill. Owen was a genuine social reformer, who initiated the first law limiting the working hours of women and children in factories. The problem was that, the more that Owen sought to generalise his philanthropic approach, the more he rubbed up against the harsh realities of the exploitative norms of capitalist organisation. When it came to selling his products in the marketplace, his egalitarianism threatened the extant rules of private property; his fair treatment of his workers threatened the authority of fellow capitalists to treat their workers less well. It was doomed to failure. As a communal experiment in the early phase of capitalism, it was a praiseworthy attempt to improve living standards, but it could not be maintained in wider society.

While Engels admired the humanity and the historical gains of the utopian socialists, he criticised their naivety. To them, he said,

[s]ociety presented nothing but wrongs; to remove these was the task of reason. It was necessary, then, to discover a new and more perfect system of social order and to impose this upon society from without by propaganda, and, wherever it was possible, by the example of model experiments. These new social systems were foredoomed as Utopian; the more completely they were worked out in detail, the more they could not avoid drifting off into pure phantasies.[50]

Modern eco-cities are just such model 'phantasies'. An interesting essay by Isabelle Whitehead draws legitimate parallels between Masdar eco-city, in Abu Dhabi in the United Arab Emirates, and the reforming industrial town of Saltaire, which opened in 1853.

Masdar is the new futuristic flagship of sustainable urbanism in the East and, like Saltaire (and many modern eco-cities), it is sponsored by industry. In Masdar's case that business is the Abu Dhabi Future Energy Company, a wholly owned subsidiary of the government's investment vehicle, the Mubadala Development Company, which is involved in oil exploration activities in Oman, Libya and south-east Asia. The town of Saltaire, in West Yorkshire, was a creation of Victorian philanthropist Sir Titus Salt, and it, too, centred around industry – his woollen mills. Masdar is designed to be zero-pollution, while Saltaire was intended to 'avoid evils so great as those resulting from polluted air and water [with] a population that would enjoy the beauties of the neighbourhood, and who would be a well-fed, contented, and happy body of operatives'. Salt's factory contained 'a tank capable of holding 500,000 gallons of rain water collected from the roofs ... which, when filtered is used in the process of manufacture'.[51] Even though Whitehead illegitimately imposes an ahistorical, non-ironic label of 'sustainability' and 'economic justice' on Saltaire, she does conclude that 'the everyday functional benefits of Saltaire and Masdar are arguably secondary to their demonstrative value as experimental showcases'.[52] Moreover, 'people's individual and group behaviour may not automatically become more sustainable just because they are placed in an "eco-friendly" built environment'.[53]

Eco-cities as defined by the *Financial Times* in the quotation at the beginning of this chapter sound very reminiscent to the ambitions and frailties of these early Victorian social reformers. In the case of New Lanark, Robert Owen believed that commercial success could be achieved without the exploitation of his workers; but modern environmental commentators make mention only of the non-exploitation of nature's resources. Two hundred years after Owen, people come a poor second. By contrast, Lord Leverhulme's model village, Port Sunlight (built in 1887) was premised on a philanthropic, welfarist agenda to improve the working conditions of its employees. Notably, it also sought to encourage the promulgation of the arts, literature, science and music. One look at the modern discourse on eco-cities is enough to establish that such cultured, humanist goals are noticeable by their absence.

Victorian capitalism closed ranks and destroyed the utopian socialists. It possessed the single-mindedness to act as a unified class in order to undermine the zeal of social reformers who threatened the social basis for capitalist profitability as they saw it. Contemporary environmentalists like to point out that, like New Lanark, many alternative environmental models in places like Dongtan are today threatened with collapse by corrupt and vested interests.

It is indeed true that the contemporary environmentalist rejection of growth would have been anathema to the majority of industrialists in the Victorian period, and would inevitably have suffered the same fate as Robert Owen. But the most significant difference between the Victorian period and today is that, rather than challenging the environmental philosophy of low growth and low aspirations as Victorians might have done, contemporary establishment figures appear not to have the necessary ideological clarity and intellectual ability to be able to do so.

Today Prince Charles, of all people, opines: 'We need to meet the challenge of decoupling economic growth from increased consumption in such a way that both the wellbeing of Nature's ecology and our own economic needs benefit simultaneously.'[54] When the future head of state says that he wants to 'make it cool *not* to use stuff',[55] it is little wonder that the British manufacturing sector is despondent. Today it is the establishment that is on the back-foot, unable (unlike in the rout of Owen) to defend itself against the new vision of limits. Modern eco-advocates who promulgate growth scepticism are today met with acceptance, applause and promotion within the corridors of power – proof positive in the flurry of eco-cities currently being built. But this curious state of affairs seems to be a sign of a lack of political will, and of defensiveness on the part of the establishment, rather than of the intellectual victory of the erstwhile eco-reformers.

Like the utopian socialist experiments, most eco-cities are little more than gated communities, isolated from outside influence. Masdar City, for example, for all its hi-tech inventions, is still a self-contained island state. While it has some fascinating gimmicks, like Norman Foster's driverless taxis, much of it is little more than an environmental version of Celebration – the model urban vision dreamed up by Disney, or Seaside, which became famous as the setting for the movie, *The Truman Show*.

Speaking of the Gulf States, US architectural critic Nicolai Ourousoff points out that, whatever their intent, such developments will inevitably 'crack the door open to some sort of Western-style modernity'.[56] Ironically, the 'walled-city' formation of many eco-cities, including Masdar, reflecting Thomas More's island Utopia, may well insulate them from outside influence for longer than might otherwise have been the case.

As eco-cities, they were designed as a safeguard against the evils of carbon-based consumerism; as a result, osmotic progress will be slower than expected. Sadly, Ourousoff may in any case be over-stating the capacity of many to defend 'Western-style modernity' in its own terms.

POSITIVE DEVELOPMENT

Utopian or not, on a positive note, the mere fact that the Middle East and Asia are building significant urban agglomerations – whether eco-prefixed or not – has a progressive kernel. Masdar, after all, is a project covering six square kilometres. Saudi Arabia's 'Economic City', housing, employing and entertaining 2 million people, is spread over 170 square kilometres. South Korea's Incheon, which is lauded as a 'self-sufficient … sustainable super-city',[57] covers over 300 square kilometres. Many of these schemes are ambitious, huge and challenging interventions designed to raise the social status, wealth and quality of life of their populations. This is probably the key distinction between the Middle Eastern and Asian version of eco-development and that of the West. That alone is worthy of praise.

However, Dongtan, an eco-city that failed in its intention to be the 'model for how to build sustainable cities worldwide'[58] should still provide a sobering lesson. And that lesson is that we need more open-mindedness, inquisitiveness and critical awareness. By blindly praising a city's environmental credentials without recognising its insularity, its compost-centric, energy-fetishising, waste-prioritising, human-isolationist, ill-considered urbanism will be a recipe for future disasters. After all, in Britain in the 1960s, the government rushed into numbers-driven housing: ill-prepared architects urged on by ill-informed contractors and an ill-judged housing policy. Then, as now, priority was given to targets, materials and technology over real people's needs. But with the more technocratic – and more risk-averse – attitude of today, the historic social problems that arose 50 years ago may come to seem mild by comparison.

NOTES

1. Richard Register, *Eco-Cities: Rebuilding Cities in Balance with Nature*, New Society Publishers, 2006, pp. xiii, 5.
2. Rodney R. White, *Building the Ecological City*, Woodhead Publishing, 2002.
3. Fiona Harvey, 'Green Vision: The Search for the Ideal Eco-City', *Financial Times*, 7 September 2010.
4. Transport for London, 'Travel in London: Key Trends and Developments: Report Number 1', TfL, p. 39.
5. Andrew Pierce, 'Buckingham Palace Tops London League Table of Least Green Buildings', *Daily Telegraph*, 11 March 2009.
6. Raj Kumar Mitra, ed., 'Trash has Crashed: Impact of Financial Crisis on Waste Pickers of Ahmedabad City', in UNDP, *Global Financial Crisis and India's Informal Economy: Review of Key Sectors*, UNDP, 2009, p. 6.
7. Eric Pickles, MP, quoted in 'Councils Dumping More Than 200,000 Tonnes of Recycling Every Year', *Daily Telegraph*, 19 December 2008.
8. Terry Cooke, 'China's Eco-Cities Initiative', *China Business Network*, 21 February 2011, at <www.thechinabusinessnetwork. com/China-s-Eco-Cities -Initiative.aspx>.
9. Francis Ayieko, 'Country's First "Eco-City" Being Built in Mombasa', *East African* (Nairobi), 29 April 2008.
10. Together Foundation, *Best Practices Database: Eco-City, Johannesburg*, UN-Habitat, 2002, p. 3.

11. Mary-Anne Toy, 'China's First Eco-Village Proves a Hard Sell', *The Age*, 26 August 2006.

12. Shannon May, 'Ecological Modernism and the Making of a New Working Class', in Adrian Parr and Michael Zaretsky, eds, *New Directions in Sustainable Design*, Routledge, 2010, pp. 37–52.

13. Shannon May, 'A US–Sino Sustainability Sham', *Far Eastern Economic Review*, April 2007, p. 58.

14. Rob Watson quoted in Danielle Sacks, 'Green Guru Gone Wrong: William McDonough', *FastCompany*, 1 November 2008, at <www.fastcompany.com/magazine/130/the-mortal-messiah.html>.

15. James Lovelock, 'James Lovelock: The Earth Is About to Catch a Morbid Fever that May Last as Long as 100,000 years', *Independent*, 16 January 2006.

16. Shannon May, 'Ecological Crisis and Eco-Villages and Eco-Cities in China', *Counterpunch*, 21–23 November 2008, at <www.counterpunch.org/may11212008.html>.

17. Yaffa Fredrick, 'The Big Question: Is There a Global Canon?' *World Policy Journal* 27: 3 (Fall 2010), pp. 3–7.

18. Julie Hill, *The Secret Life of Stuff: A Manual for a New Material World*, Vintage Originals, 2011, p. 4.

19. McKenzie Funk, 'China's Green Evolution', *Popular Science*, August 2007, p. 114.

20. Leah Lamb, 'China's Eco-Cities Bridge Fantasy with Reality?' *National Geographic* NatGeo NewsWatch, 23 June 2010, at <blogs.nationalgeographic.com/blogs/news/chiefeditor/2010/06/china-Eco-Cities.html>.

21. Fred Pearce, 'The Population Bomb: Has It Been Defused?' *Yale Environment 360*, 11 August 2008, at <e360.yale.edu/content/feature.msp?id=2042>.

22. Alex Steffen, 'Dongtan and Greening China', WorldChanging.com, 1 May 2006, at <www.worldchanging.com/archives/004378.html>.

23. Paul French quoted in Christina Larson, 'China's Grand Plans for Eco-Cities Now Lie Abandoned', *Yale Environment 360*, 6 April 2009, at <e360.yale.edu/content/feature.msp?id=2138>.

24. Tatsuo Inoue, 'Liberal Democracy and Asian Orientalism', in Joanne R. Bauer and Daniel A. Bell, eds, *The East Asian Challenge for Human Rights*, CUP, 1999, p. 39.

25. Dustin R. Turin, 'China and the Beijing Consensus: An Alternative Model for Development', *Student Pulse* 2: 1 (January 2010), p. 2.

26. Jasper Becker, *Hungry Ghosts: Mao's Secret Famine*, Free Press, 1997.

27. Kent G. Deng, *Globalisation: Today, Tomorrow*, Sciyo, 2010, p. 145.

28. Martin Ravallion, 'Are There Lessons for Africa from China's Success Against Poverty?' *World Development* 37: 2 (2009), p. 307.

29. Simon Joss, *Eco-Cities: A Global Survey 2009; Part A: Eco-City Profiles*, *Governance and Sustainability*, University of Westminster, 2010, p. 35.

30. Pamela Buxton, 'China Blueprint', *RIBA Journal*, 27 August 2009.

31. Roger Wood, 'Dongtan Eco-City, Shanghai', presentation, Planning Institute of Australia, National Congress, Perth, Western Australia, 4 May 2007.

32. Tylene Levesque, 'RIZHAO: China's Solar-Powered Sunshine City', *Inhabitat*, 5 June 2007, at <inhabitat.com/rizhao-the-sunshine-city>.

33. C. J. Lim quoted in 'Chinese Eco-City', University College London press release, 23 March 2007, at <www.ucl.ac.uk/news/news-articles/0703/07032301>.

34. Joss, *Eco-Cities: A Global Survey 2009*, p. 35.

35. Caofedian New District Management Committee, 'China Caofeidian New District: General View', at <en.cfdxq.gov.cn/GeneralContentShow/&contentid=86a13857-7acb-4cc4-bb52-e9e6cfc7522d&comp_stats=comp-FrontCommonContent_showTree-123.html>.

36. Qiang Ma, 'Eco-City and Eco-Planning in China: Taking an Example for Caofeidian Eco-City', in The 4th International Conference of the International Forum on Urbanism (IFoU), *The New Urban Question: Urbanism Beyond Neo-Liberalism*, Amsterdam/Delft, 2009, p. 519.

37. Xia Huan, 'Tangshan: From Earthquake to Eco-City', *China Daily*, 31 July 2008.

38. Jessie Tao, 'Caofeidian: A Shining Star in North China', *China Daily*, 1 March 2006.

39. Shell, 'Pearl GTL: An Overview', at <www.shell.com/home/content/
     aboutshell/our_strategy/major_projects_2/pearl/overview>.
40. Kim Kwi-Gon and Kim Kweesoon, 'Sustainable Cities and Korean
     Ecological Tradition', *Korea Journal*, August 1999, p. 144.
41. Constitution of the Communist Party Of China (Amended and
     Adopted at the Seventeenth National Congress of the Communist
     Party of China on 21 October 2007), General Program, Foreign
     Languages Press, 2007.
42. Li Xing, 'Growth is Good But It Must Be Green', *China Daily*,
     26 March 2009.
43. Erich W. Schienke, 'The Green Edge', in Neville Mars and Adrian
     Hornsby, eds, *The Chinese Dream: A Society Under Construction*',
     010 Publishers, p. 154.
44. Campaign to Protect Rural England, 'Eco-Towns: Threat or
     Opportunity?' 14 February 2008, at <www.cpre.org.uk/news/
     view/471>.
45. Gordon Brown quoted in Tania Branigan, 'Brown Sets Out to
     Woo Back Middle England', *Guardian*, 14 May 2007.
46. 'China Adopts 5-Year Blueprint, Aiming for Fairer, Greener
     Growth', *People's Daily Online*, 14 March 2011, at <www.
     chinadaily.com.cn/xinhua/2011-03-14/content_2012745.html>.
47. Sino-Singapore Tianjin Eco-City, 'Celebrating Eco', Investment
     and Development Co., p. 2.
48. Fredrich Engels, *The Condition of the Working-Class in England
     in 1844*, George Allen & Unwin, 1943, p. 54.
49. Tristram Hunt, *The Frock-Coated Communist: The Revolutionary
     Life of Friedrich Engels*, Allen Lane, 2009, p. 80.
50. Friedrich Engels, *Socialism: Utopian and Scientific*, Cosimo, Inc.,
     2008, p. 36
51. R. Balgarnie, *Sir Titus Salt, Baronet: His Life and Its Lessons*,
     Hodder & Stoughton, 1877, pp. 82–4.
52. Isabelle Whitehead, 'Models of Sustainability? A Comparative
     Analysis of Ideal City Planning in Saltaire and Masdar City',
     School of Geosciences, University of Sydney, 2010, p. 2.
53. Ibid., p. 6.
54. HRH The Prince of Wales, 'Wasting Nature's Capital Means
     Financial Ruin', *The Times*, 9 February 2011.

55. David Derbyshire, '"Stop Playing Roulette with the Future": Prince Charles Blasts Big Business on Climate Change', *Daily Mail*, 10 February 2011.

56. Nicolai Ourousoff, 'Saudi Urban Projects Are a Window to Modernity', *New York Times*, 12 December 2010.

57. Katie Scott, 'South Korea Plans Sustainable Super City', *Wired*, 1 September 2009.

58. Herbert Girardet, 'Which way China?' *China Dialogue*, 2 October 2006, at <www.chinadialogue.net/article/show/single/en/297-Which-way-China->.

8
The Visionary City
Things Will Endure Less than Us

Austin Williams and Karl Sharro

People make their own cities, but never under the conditions of their own choosing.

Roy Porter, *London: A Social History*

The Futurist movement was conceived out of a haze of drink-fuelled rhetoric at the cusp of the First World War. Its founder, the Italian Filippo Tommaso Marinetti, wrote its manifesto in 1909, which spoke of a love of machines, speed, flight, youth, dynamism and of 'ruinous and incendiary violence'.[1] The Futurists celebrated change and spontaneity; they were contemptuous of old ways and wished to challenge rather than accommodate to nature. There was no place for sleep. Driving his car into a ditch, after failing to hit some cyclists, Marinetti was invigorated by the danger. Theirs was a risk-taking mindset. As artists, sculptors, essayists, designers and poets, they opened up a challenge to the world, to consciousness and to the established order. It was, says author Alex Danchev, an 'adventure of artistic expression'.[2]

Fast-forward 100 years and, by comparison there is no discourse except the droning mantra of sustainability, conservation and playfulness. While architecture is enjoying a resurgence in the media, in its intellectual guise it has never been more vacuous, pliant, parochial or insular.[3] Le Corbusier criticised the architecture of his age as 'strewn with the detritus of old dead epochs' and advanced the idea that 'movement is the law of our existence: nothing ever stands still', while one author (discussed in Chapters 1 and 9) proclaimed that '[t]he future … wages a ceaseless war against the monuments of the past'.[4]

Whatever you may think of these and other Modernist radicals' political objectives, nowhere today do we hear such challenging sentiments. In fact, modern-day architecture is complacent by comparison, its edifice shaken only by self-doubt. Where Modernism represented the architectural machine age, today we have only a mechanistic approach to architecture

In such a vapid political age in the West, maybe this is hardly surprising. But more worryingly, social commentators and practitioners of architecture and urbanism display no collective sense of outrage at this vacuum. When Marinetti was 56, long after his self-proclaimed sell-by date, he was still pushing Dada-esque boundaries with his *Futurist Cookbook* of 1932. Even that cultural manifesto was a satirical challenge to the system, but Futurism's only role today, it seems, is to be resuscitated as a nostalgic piss-take. On the anniversary of the original manifesto, in 2009, chefs offered Marinetti's 'chicken with ball bearings' and kumqats served with sandpaper and silk in reverential silence. But there was no significant historical-cultural rationale. Marinetti would have been outraged.

In the sixties, Archigram experimented with ideas such as the 'Plug-in-City', the 'Walking City' and the 'Instant City'. None of those ideas were ever built, but Archigram became one of the most influential sources of architectural thinking until the present day.[5] Archigram's work was a product of a decade of technological optimism and the pursuit of individual freedoms, both of which it encapsulated. By contrast, in the West today we seem to adopt a more pessimistic view of the future while we become increasingly preoccupied with limits to our aspirations. This sharp turn in outlook has had its impact on how we imagine and think about cities.

This chapter seeks to explore the changing face of visionary urbanism. How could a century that offered radical visions of the city, ranging from the sensible but ambitious to the science-fiction,[6] end in an almost total acceptance of the nineteenth century as the main model for how we think about the design of cities?[7]

Of course, this attitude predominantly reflects the prevailing thinking in Europe and America; in places like China, India, Brazil and the Arabian Gulf a renewed appetite for development is leading to massive transformations. But the pace of change in these places is often met with apprehension in the West, reflecting a lack of appetite for change. Western scepticism about the rapid rise 'over there' – in the 'emerging economies' – reflects disenchantment with the idea of progress 'over here'.

If there are visionary cities to be found today, they are either ironic products of a nostalgic attitude to the past, engineering gimmickry, or embodiments of the uncertainties of our age. In what follows we will examine some of the retreats from urban reason that have kept visionary architecture alive (if only on a pacemaker), and look at the impact of the absence of visionary thinking on one of the fastest-growing cities in the world. Finally, we explore the rise and fall of ideological dynamism.

MODERNISM'S PROMISE AND PROMISE DENIED

'*Visionary* when coupled with *architecture* implies something fantastic … More than merely innovative, the word suggests provocative, critical work that not only explains present conditions but reveals a preferred – sometimes astonishing – future.'[8]

Every graphic depiction of a visionary city has embodied an attitude about man's relationship to society, nature and the past – and, of course, the future. The visionary city served as a testing platform for the social imagination and how it could reconceive the human condition. It matters very little whether a particular vision is realised; what matters much more are the possibilities that it opens up, the influence it exerts on our thinking, and its ability to encapsulate social aspirations.

The Italian architect Sant'Elia's masterful sketches of visionary, idealistic and technically exciting 'Cities of the Future' are still regarded by many as highly ambitious. Fantastical and beautiful, they speak of the future, but also retain a dark quality that seems to foreshadow – as with many visionaries of his generation –

his death in the First World War, which robbed us of the fully realised potential of some of the great innovative and creative minds of the period.

Sant'Elia's Città Nuova was predicated on electric power, skyscrapers, pedestrian precincts and traffic moving on overhead roadways at two and three different levels, imagined at a time when motorised transport was just becoming a mass-produced reality, and a mere ten years after the first powered flight. His *Futurist Manifesto of Architecture* (*Manifesto dell'Architettura Futurista*), printed in August 1914, states that 'the street will no longer lie like a doormat at ground level, but will plunge many stories down into the earth, embracing the metropolitan traffic, and will be linked up for necessary interconnections by metal gangways and swift-moving pavements'.[9]

Le Corbusier also proposed the city on many levels, as a three-dimensional chess board. Author David Ohana describes how, 'in the centre of the city were several levels of traffic, one above the other, and the top level was a landing strip for aeroplanes, and the central railway station was below it'.[10] These were radical plans that were beginning to be thought of as possible, rather than utopian projects. Science and technological advances were already starting to spark the imagination. In his seminal but critical work on Modernism, Professor Ohana notes that Corbusier was offended when his 'Plan for a Contemporary City of Three Million Inhabitants' was labelled a 'City of the Future'. As someone caught up in transforming the now, he did not want to wait. Writing in 1920, Alexander Rodchenko, the Russian Contructivist photographer wrote: 'I am so interested in the future, that I want to be able to see several years ahead right away.' He went on to insist that 'it is our duty to experiment'.

With such a place in history, with such vigour, excitement and urgency, it is right that the UK's Victoria and Albert Museum recognised that '[t]he built environment that we live in today was largely shaped by Modernism ... We live in an era that still identifies itself in terms of Modernism, as post-Modernist or even post-post-Modernist.'[11] Modernism is so intrinsically bound up with the early twentieth century that it can only be appreciated within the context of the era: a period of tumult in which Modernism's chief intervention was to claim the future and reject the past.

The weight of Modernism's legacy still exerts a disproportionate influence on the practice and theory of urbanism today. The Modernists' willingness to experiment with new ideas and reject inherited forms and traditions represented a substantial break from the past that seems out of place in the more cautious world we now occupy. It is true that there are those who champion Modernism loudly, but only as a historical curiosity that should be confined to museums. In that, its champions differ very little from its critics: Modernism is treated as an aesthetic style[12] to be loved or hated, but not as a representation of a social attitude towards architecture and the city that embraces change and experimentation.

It is of course only natural to see a dimension of social engineering within Modernism's approach; after all, social control was one of its implied aims. But it is also very easy to exaggerate the role of this aspect of Modernism from our contemporary vantage point. The Modernist ethos was aspirational; architects like Le Corbusier were concerned with solving society's problems through the use of technology and the production of new architecture and cities that reflected the machine age. In most instances, this focus chimed with the wider aspirations of society itself, and with its pursuit of progress. The visionary dimension was evident in the Modernist architects' willingness to imagine radically different ways of organising society and space. It would be absurd to pretend that those visions were realised comprehensively; but in many instances they served to test out new ideas and explore the boundaries of possibility. Some of the reactions today to Le Corbusier's 1924 'Plan Voisin' for Paris seem intentionally to miss the point of his exercise. The plan proposed wiping out large sections of central Paris and replacing them with cruciform towers interspersed with parks and gardens. Le Corbusier's plan was true to the spirit of provocative visionary cities: it explored new ideas and rejected the dominance of the past. Taking the plan literally misses the point.

MODERN NOSTALGIA

It is important to locate the debate about the future of the city against the backdrop of an intellectual climate increasingly defined by a preoccupation with the idea of limits and scepticism towards growth. Tim Jackson, UK government advisor and professor of sustainable development at the University of Sydney, articulated this stance as follows: 'The vision of social progress that drives us – based on the continual expansion of material wants – is fundamentally untenable. And this failing is not a simple falling short from utopian ideals.'[13]

Jackson's book *Prosperity Without Growth: Economics for a Finite Planet* is one of a large number of texts that encapsulate the idea of limits and argue for a move away from the pursuit of material wealth. And while this idea is certainly taking hold in the West, it is worth noting that it resonates with many across the world. The Singaporean environmentalist Chandran Nair made a similar case against Asian expansion in his book *Consumptionomics: Asia's Role in Reshaping Capitalism and Saving the Planet*. His message is phrased rather more bluntly:

> We need to rethink policies and political action, about how we define growth, wealth creation, what we can do and own, and how we should work and live. We must question the assumption that everyone in Asia should aspire to own a car, live and work in air-conditioned surroundings, and consume food and goods shipped from every corner of the world.[14]

This is more than protectionism. Both Jackson's and Nair's theses, replicated by commentators across the world, tend to emphasise qualitative factors and challenge the importance of material prosperity. Fundamentally, both commentators – much like critics of growth in general – gloss over the fact that housing, education, health and employment all require investments in modern urban infrastructure and development.

Prescribing a ceiling for this type of development in response to perceived limits to growth translates into a lowering of expectations, as Nair clearly states. But the very essence of visionary urbanism, and therefore the urgent challenge we face today in its absence, consists in its transcending of those artificial limits that represent the limits to social imagination (rather than reflecting actual physical limits).

With the world moving into the 'Urban Age' – with more than half of the world's population now living in cities,[15] and a new generation of mega-cities emerging – it is worth challenging the dominance that the traditional city enjoys over the urban imagination, and refuting the notion that it should represent the template for the future of urban life. At the same time, it is important that we challenge the idea that there are inherent limits that would stifle such an expansion of cities. Instead, we should ask whether we can design cities in a different way that ensures that the gains we have made in personal mobility, housing standards and quality of life can be maintained and improved upon, so that everyone in the world can enjoy the life standards that are the norm in the West. Visionary urbanism should be reclaimed as an inquisitive and speculative discipline that can experiment with new ideas to explore ways of achieving these aims.

Undoubtedly, rather than a modernising alternative stretching urbanists' imagination, we are stuck with a rootedness in the safety of the past. Instead of taking a leap of faith in society's – and humanity's – ability to cope and revel in redefining and reinventing places (see Chapter 5), there is a womb-like embrace of comfortable, established norms. This culminates in western commentators' inability to comprehend the tendency for emerging economies not to show the same conservatism. Clinging to 'the detritus of old, dead epochs' is less politically expedient in more dynamic parts of the world. Back in the West, architects and urbanists project their visions of the future from the sanctuary of the past – but a sanitized version of the past that has been cleansed of any unpleasant associations.

According to Hans Stimmann, the planner who in effect remodelled post-unification Berlin, 'Progress in architecture does not come from breaking away from time-tested traditions, typologies and techniques, but from developing them further.'[16] Quoted in the *New York Times* discussing his first days on the job, in 1991, he recalled, 'I had a drawer and I opened it up and pulled out the old city plan ... I said: "It worked for 250 years. Why do we need a new competition?"[17]

Berlin is a fascinating case study. It is a city trying to come to terms with its uncomfortable history; and yet, instead of being inspired to create a new urban vision, it has led instead to urbanists having to dig further back to locate a safe period from which to locate themselves. Such opportunism would not be so surprising if it was just that the arch-traditionalist, Stimmann, was saying it. But David Chipperfield, RIBA Gold Medal winner and designer of a significant number of landmark buildings in Berlin, is a self-declared Modernist, and sounds remarkably similar. He too harks back to the values of Classicism: from his Neues Museum and Am Kupfergraben gallery in Berlin to his Folkwang Museum in Essen and Stirling Prize–winning Museum of Modern Literature in Marbach am Neckar, in Baden-Württemberg. He declares that the early Modernists ignored the 'established history of forms', creating a 'disconnection with history', and he hopes that the tools of Classicism can be reclaimed and 'reassume their innocence'.[18] He craves the sanctuary of 'normality'. Not the most radical *cri de cœur* of the Modernist; in fact, it is a rejection of the substantive meaning of the word Modernism in order to give way to a stylistic, pick-and-mix approach. Modernism, shorn of its transformative kernel, is Modernism denuded. This is 'Modern' architecture that earns the name simply by virtue of having been designed recently.

Adolf Loos is widely recognised as a transitional figure in the early decades of twentieth-century Modernism. The great architectural historian Banister Fletcher said of him that he 'never repudiated Classicism'.[19] Coming from a crafts background, Loos turned his attention to functionalism and form after visiting the Chicago World's Fair at the age of 23, becoming an unabashed Modern figure who was best known as a polemicist and 'agent provocateur'. It is reasonable to explain his shifting allegiances on the basis of the unformed ideas constituting the first stirrings of Modernism. Irene Murray, co-curator of the 2011 Royal Institute of British Architects' exhibition of his work, says that 'he would be the first to admit and then repudiate that he contradicted himself at every turn'.[20]

Fundamentally, Modernism was a break with the past. The Modernist rift has certainly confused establishment figures for 100 years. Roger Scruton bemoans the fact that the modern destroyed tradition. That is true. Indeed, the revolutionary zeal that initiated many of Modernism's cityscapes created a cultural missing link in the evolution of urban history – which was unfortunate, but was also the point. It was meant to be a radical shift that would take society forward, not back. The Dutch architect Rem Koolhaas is contemptuous of the nostalgia towards the traditional city: 'For urbanists, the belated rediscovery of the virtues of the classical city [means that] they are now specialists in phantom pain: doctors discussing the medical intricacies of an amputated limb.'[21] But Koolhaas has come to represent another dominant school of thought in urbanism – one that is problematic in its own right. It is one that tends to shy away from totalising or universal visions:

> If there is to be a 'new urbanism' it will not be based on the twin fantasies of order and omnipotence; it will be the staging of uncertainty; it will no longer be concerned with the arrangement of more or less permanent objects but with the irrigation of territories with potential.[22]

But the idea of order is central to how we think about the city and society. The 'staging of uncertainty' is a euphemism for refusing to impose order on the world around us. Visionary cities, from Plato onwards, were always concerned with questions about the nature of this order, and about imposing order on nature. Koolhaas's formulation is pragmatic: it allows designers the space to intervene in the city without being tied down by ideological constraints or being concerned with responding to the deeper questions about what shape life in the city should take. Koolhaas knows that he disapproves of the romantic reclamation of Modernism, but neither does he have anything to offer in its place:

> Modernism's alchemistic promise – to transform quantity into quality through abstraction and repetition – has been a failure, a hoax: magic that didn't work. Its ideas, aesthetics, strategies are finished. Together, all attempts to make a new beginning have only discredited the idea of a new beginning. A collective shame in the wake of this fiasco has left a massive crater in our understanding of modernity and modernization.[23]

Clearly, these are the earnest criticisms of a demoralised and disorientated man; but as such they absolve the discipline of the responsibility for engaging in visionary thinking. His argument is largely based on his assessment of Modernism's failure to fulfil its promise. He is not unique in that respect.

RETREATS FROM REASON

Demoralisation is nothing new. But today's philosophical retreat arises from a generalised fear of the future, of growth, of humanity's hubris, of risk. In the mid-twentieth century, demoralisation tended to result from society's failure to deliver. Vision was undulled; it was just that its advocates were demoralised politically. Along the way, there have been some highly imaginative, visionary cities – but cities that have sought to manufacture an escape from reality. Although they display architectural merit, design innovation and futuristic rhetoric, they are effectively retreats from reason.

Auroville in Pondicherry, on the south-east coast of India, is a classic case in point – a retreat in every sense of the word. For over 50 years it has been a 'city-in-the-making' peopled with Western escapists, retreatists and travellers. It has long hoped to grow to 50,000 residents, but in fact it has reached a plateau of 2,000 people, living in 100 settlements of varying size. Although there is an interesting mix of nationalities represented – from over 30 countries – this is not a city, and will never reach its goal of being one, precisely because its existence represents an escape from the city.

Similarly, Arcosanti, 70 miles north of metropolitan Phoenix, Arizona, is a futuristic urban dreamscape created by architect

Paolo Soleri. In 1961, his plans for a city of 2 million people were included in the Museum of Modern Art's exhibition, *Visionary Architecture*.[24] His plan was, and remains, to construct a new model of living in the Arizona desert. Begun in 1970, it is nowhere near being finished.

Soleri interned with Frank Lloyd Wright at Taliesin, but he turned his attention from Modernism to 'arcology' – his word for a combination of architecture and ecology. For 40 years he has dug himself into the desert – creating compact structures and large-scale solar greenhouses that occupy just 25 acres of a 4,060 acre land preserve.[25]

In recent years, with the growth of the environmental mainstream, Arcosanti has received some of the attention that it previously lacked, but it still remains an oddity rather than a desirable model of living. According to Jeffrey Cook, a professor of architecture at Arizona State Universitys: 'He was part of a flock of utopian dreamers who designed megastructure cities in the 1960s, but he had more of a social and ecological agenda than the others. His arguments continue to hold water.'[26] Indeed, one of the handful of long-term residents explains the original intent. He would 'build up, not out', rejecting suburban sprawl and reducing the need for automobiles in a self-contained community. It has always relied on the labour of students (*à la* Taliesin), among whom working on the project is viewed as an internship – in a kibbutz-style campus or an ashram retreat – rather than representing any long-term commitment. Indeed, it aims to be a city of 5,000 people, but continues to be a never-ending building site of reasonably unattractive concrete shells: its permanent construction has become the sole rationale for its existence. Even arch-environmentalist Alex Steffen recognised the sterility of the place, noting that 'Arcosanti isn't the future anymore. It smells too much of museum dust. It's the embalmed husk of a future, and a future that's older than I am, at that. I get in my car, and drive back down the rutted road, and wonder if I'll find some fresher dream ahead.'[27]

Both Auroville and Arcosanti were clear responses to the 1960s, and both were religious – one overtly, the other covertly. But both emanated from a cultural milieu that wanted something more, something different. That embryonic positive instinct was subverted into an 'alternative' lifestyle to create a parallel universe, rather than trying to change the actual universe for the better. It is ultimately defeatist, and cannot compare with the Modernist agenda of – and attempts at – changing the world that they found so disagreeable.

The other visionary urban conception of the last 50 years is one that sums up the essence of visionary architecture: it is space habitation. From *Flash Gordon* to *Star Trek*, space exploration embodied the excitement of the New World – the New Frontier. Even back then, space urbanism therefore seemed more like a science-fiction proposal than a serious proposition, but it was taken seriously by major institutes, funders and academic bodies. Rooted in the Space Age of the Kennedy era, and popularised by Kubrick, space was then a viable ambition.

One such urban project was the 'Stanford Torus' (named after Stanford University, where it was originally devised). It was proposed in 1975 as a space habitat for between 10,000 and 140,000 people, to include men, women and children as well as domesticated and farmed animals. It was a huge doughnut-shaped wheel, 1.8 kilometres in diameter, which rotated to create earth-like gravitational conditions around its inner circumference, where the people would live and work. Physicist Gerard O'Neill's groundbreaking book *The High Frontier: Human Colonies in Space* (including Pierre Mion's beautiful colour illustrations representing life aboard the floating space station) caught the public's imagination, and O'Neill was hailed as a spokesman for the space-colonisation movement, which predicted a future for these vast, inhabited space communities. Space pioneers would survive by mining the lunar surface, building more space stations for successive communities to live among the stars. This, surely, is the stuff of progressive visionary architecture? It promised a dynamic human-centred ownership of the twenty-first century, and suggested that human-controlled technology would be our salvation.

And there's the rub – its objective was 'human salvation'. The space-colonisation movement became too closely associated with the need to flee a world heading towards imminent mutually assured destruction. It was hugely ambitious in scale and other practicalities, but still grounded in an earthly demoralisation and desire for escapism. As space historian Dwayne Day points out, 'It didn't make many converts. There was a problem with [its] vision: it was not inherently positive and uplifting. There were certainly many negative visions at the time: Malthusian predictions of doom, and the ever-present fear of nuclear annihilation.'[28]

Like Soleri burying himself in the sands of Arizona, space represented mere survivalism – though of a more high-tech nature. Once again, the very logic of the enterprise was its downfall, fed as it was by the perceived need to flee the planet to avoid man-made disaster. It was not such a leap of imagination to begin worrying about whether an untried space station might equally be a man-made disaster waiting to happen. Nervous questions were asked about the devastating consequences of space fragments piercing the shell. If you build an urban vision on paranoia, then it is hardly surprising when people get paranoid.

The ambition of secure space habitation offering a terrestrial quality of life is eminently appealing, and its overtones are as futuristic today as ever before – if not more so. Though China is reported to have plans to build a lunar station by 2020, the prospect of cities on the moon remains the stuff of science fiction. 'The Future', says Day, 'it was wonderful, but now it survives largely in the pages of faded magazines'.[29]

THE NEW 'VISIONARY' CITIES

Back on terra firma, or at least on the shifting sands of the Middle East, the Arabian Gulf has increased in dynamism in recent times, and the cities developing there have become a testing ground for architectural ideas and technologies. It is hard not to register the disciplinary apathy of architecture and urbanism in the West towards those cities. The lack of serious academic study is one side of this apathy, but it is also expressed in the absence of any vision that could capitalise on this energy and dynamism to create innovative cities and urban typologies.

Rem Koolhaas's design for the 1.5-billion-square-foot Waterfront City development in Dubai is probably the only serious 'high-brow' proposal for Dubai, and aims to simulate Manhattan's density there. Borrowing an existing model and implanting it in Dubai, it consciously avoids the temptation to slip into utopianism. It is ironic that Koolhaas, who criticised urbanists for attempting to revive the classical city, would revert to a similar attitude by simulating Manhattan's fabric. The 'found' city in this instance is presented as less contentious than a speculative 'visionary' city. It is worth asking, however, whether this represents anything more than a tactic to avoid the work of re-imagining the city.

It is of course naive to separate the subject of the visionary city from its socio-political context. At the heart of the question of what kind of cities we want to live in are those of what kind of society we aspire to and what our ideals are. The lack of visionary thinking in urbanism is a reflection of the lack of progressive political ideas that embrace development and the desire to fulfil our human potential. In the absence of such projects, it is no surprise that societies with more concentrated power are proving to be more dynamic and more capable of bringing about economic development.

During the last decade, Dubai has become a symbol for aggressive growth and expansion, as illustrated by the miles of skyscrapers along its central thoroughfare, Sheikh Zayed Road. Crucially, it also developed into a regional industrial centre. While some argue that it has already experienced deindustrialisation,[30] it is more accurate to say that it is undergoing a managed transition from labour intensive, low-technology industries to capital intensive, advanced-technology industries.[31]

Many of Dubai's critics like to point out that it is unplanned, and that it is merely an assemblage of individual, hastily erected monuments. But such an assessment, seeing the entire city as a kind of vanity project,[32] seems to be a superficial observation based on the inability of such observers to cope with its constantly changing geography and skyline. In fact, Dubai's recent growth was planned according to the 1993 Urban Area Structure Plan,[33] which anticipated that 90 per cent of Dubai's urban area would be developed by 2015.[34] Dubai's fast growth and economic diversification have set a precedent that other cities in the region, such as Doha, Riyadh and Abu Dhabi, are keen to emulate. While it is easy to dismiss some of Dubai's more outlandish buildings as kitschy, Dubai presents a dilemma for urbanists. It represents the antithesis of the contemporary ideas that they are championing, and it does not resemble any of the readymade conceptual models they have developed to understand cities. Perhaps this motivates the dismissive attitude displayed towards it by people like architect and theorist Lebbeus Woods: 'As an unregulated sanctuary for cash – it has no depth of history or indigenous culture, no complexity, no conflicts, no questions about itself, no doubts, in short, nothing to stand in the way of its being shaped into the ultimate neo-liberal Utopia.'[35]

The lack of 'genuine urban conditions' is a recurring theme in discussions about Dubai, but it is hard to square this with its recent growth and dynamism. It is likely that this judgement stems from direct comparisons between Dubai and cities like Paris or London, but this begs the question of why the traditional European city should be used as the model against which emerging cities should be understood. Dubai is certainly distinct from European cities, and there are real lessons – positive ones – to be learned. But the implication here is that Dubai is lacking in 'authenticity' – another recurring theme in urban readings of the city. Another influential thinker, the American urban theorist Mike Davis, also emphasises the idea of Dubai's 'artificiality' as a central theme in his critique:

> The elite of transnational engineering firms and retail developers are invited to plug in high-tech clusters, entertainment zones, artificial islands, glass-domed 'snow mountains', *Truman Show* suburbs, cities within cities – whatever is big enough to be seen from space and bursting with architectural steroids.[36]

Davis's article about Dubai was republished in an edited collection entitled *Evil Paradises*,[37] the title of which sums up the attitude of many academics towards Dubai. The moralistic

prism through which Dubai is viewed partially explains the lack
of serious academic studies of Dubai's urban development.

When it comes to Dubai, urbanists lament its lack of public
space and argue that it is made of singular objects, not as an
urban fabric along the traditional European model. In fact, the
least successful projects for Dubai and other cities in the Gulf are
the ones that try to reproduce this Western model, with its dense
low- and medium-rise buildings, public squares and green spaces.
This approach fails to appreciate both the local conditions that
influence Dubai's urban morphology and the fact that Dubai
has created a new urban typology that is different from more
traditional models. This is not without precedent; when Le
Corbusier visited New York in the 1930s he was extremely
distressed with what he saw.[38] Manhattan's skyscrapers seemed
to be the antithesis of his ideas; they paid no attention to his
purist aesthetic principles, and were closely jammed together,
omitting green spaces in between that he had envisaged. He
failed to see that Manhattan was developing into a unique
architectural and urban model that obeyed a different logic to the
one he had imagined. As Yasser Elsheshtawy, associate professor
of architecture at UAE University, puts it, Dubai

> is an Arab success story, an example of successful urbanisation that has
> eluded other parts of the region; it is also a good model for transnational
> urbanism, i.e. the degree to which, seemingly, it has been able to integrate
> various ethnic groups in a multi-cultural setting (labour camps notwith-
> standing). And it also has become a source of great influence in the region
> – to the extent that the so-called Dubai model became an actual term,
> connoting the exportability of its particular mode of development.[39]

Despite the fact that Dubai's development has been driven by
overly centralised political power, it has still managed to achieve
an advanced level of urbanisation, and it is not crippled by any
of the aesthetic or ideological restraints that now pass for good
judgement in urban design circles. Furthermore, it is flexible,
and thus able to respond to change in ways that rigidly planned
cities would not be.

Dubai's elevated metro network, by no means the first, is one solution that maximises the use of three-dimensional space to allow for more efficient transport. While we may have grown accustomed in the West to the idea that rationing mobility is the only feasible option, the visionary option would be to capitalise on three-dimensional movement to maintain mobility in dense cities. This is reminiscent, but not a facsimile, of Sant'Elia's century-old vision.

The idea of Dubai as a visionary city – a 'space city in the desert' – is not universally accepted, but in the absence of grand visions elsewhere it certainly stands out in that respect. It is true that Dubai can be shocking and alienating, especially to the first-time visitor, but those were once desirable qualities for the avant-garde. This experience of Dubai exemplifies 'the shock of the new', and also has a significant transformative potential on cities in the region. The story is repeated across the region in cities like Manama, Muscat and Riyadh, which are experiencing significant growth in areas varying from finance to heavy industry.

But it is not all plain sailing; in Qatar, for example, concepts from traditional Qatari architecture are 'reinterpreted' and 'reintroduced' into the modern development, in an attempt to 'establish an architectural language that is unique to Doha'.[40] The design guidelines emphasise the need to 'reflect Qatari architectural heritage while keeping an eye on the future'.[41] The result is a hybrid that relies too much on formal nods to tradition while not projecting much about the future. As one reviewer put it, 'Musheireb … looks back, not to a golden age of prosperity, but to what preceded it. If only it would try a bit harder to look forwards.'[42] This sentiment could equally apply to visionary urbanism today: Why not try harder to look forwards?

RECLAIMING THE FUTURE

The most influential urban idea in the West today is undoubtedly that of the 'compact city', which seems to have become its default city model. Architect Richard Rogers is one of its most prominent advocates, and he has written several books about it and based the recommendations of the Urban Task Force, *Towards an Urban Renaissance*,[43] on its model. The idea of the 'compact city' broadly advocates limiting car use and green-field development, encouraging the recycling of land, and promoting dense city developments, as well as walking and cycling. It reflects the environmental anxieties that dominate public debate these days, but it also represents a form of nostalgia for a more traditional city form. More extreme variations have emerged as a result of survival having become a central theme in how we think about cities, as in the case of C. J. Lim's 'smart-cities'.[44] Lim's approach focuses on integrating agriculture within the city, and is represented through futuristic architectural imagery. But he also argues that agriculture can play an increased role in building social cohesion. Lim's vision is even more backward-looking than that of Rogers, seeking a form of spiritual salvation in agriculture.

Ideas like the 'compact city' and Koolhaas's 'enabling fields' – territories that stage uncertainty – largely prescribe the parameters within which urbanism is understood today. The former sees the role of urbanism as responding to social and environmental problems that are perceived as limits to human activity, while the latter sees it as a facilitator for urban processes, rather than as a master-narrative. They both represent limits to visionary thinking. One sees the *tabula rasa* as human encroachment on nature, while the other sees it as a futile attempt to coordinate social interaction. The theme of limits is common: natural limits, human limits and limits to the imagination. In many ways, it is the idea of limits itself that represents one of the most intractable obstacles to visionary thinking today. Real visionary thinking, by definition, seeks to overcome perceived limits and to open up new possibilities.

Whether you agree with them or not, the original, true avant-garde produced original thinkers, rebels and radicals trying to revolutionise our responses to the deadening hand of conservative thinking and in favour of freedom of expression. One hundred years ago, Adolf Loos's rebel yell, 'Ornament is crime', created a stir that has still not subsided. Today's whimper, 'CO2 is crime', has instead generated blind acceptance.

While the impact of tradition on the way we think about cities today manifests itself strongly in formal influences on projects like Masdar and Musheireb, it also affects the way we look at cities in the West. Today it seems that we can only contemplate the past with a sense of its weight on our shoulders. Every action we take is restricted somehow by a bygone era and its physical legacy, as cities increasingly embrace the logic of preservation.

If visionary thinking is to take a leading role again, the logic of restraint, the predilection for small-scale interventions and the dominance of traditional models must all be challenged. Even by the logic of those who advocate an attitude that places risks and challenges at the centre of our thinking about architecture and urbanism, we are more likely to succeed if we adopt bold and ambitious strategies rather than half-hearted measures. But that requires us to overcome a significant limitation: our apprehension and anxiety about the future. These reflect the widespread cultural pessimism that afflicts our thinking. Preserving the gains of civilisation should also be a central aim; after all, we could get by with very little if we scaled down our ambitions significantly. Ironically, it is the ideas that champion this scaling-down of ambition that have come to monopolise visionary thinking today; but it is a dim vision that they project.

Perhaps the idea of a new beginning ought to be resurrected, and with it our capacity to re-imagine the city. To be visionary, we must learn to look at the future with excitement once again. We leave the last word to Sant'Elia: 'From an architecture conceived in this way no formal or linear habit can grow, since the fundamental characteristics of Futurist architecture will be its impermanence and transience. Things will endure less than us. Every generation must build its own city.'

NOTES

1. Filippo Tommaso Marinetti, 'The Futurist Manifesto', originally published in French, in *Le Figaro*, Paris, 20 February 1909.

2. Alex Danchev, '100 Artists' Manifestos', Penguin Classics, 2011.

3. Alastair Donald, Richard J. Williams, Karl Sharro, Alan Farlie, Debby Kuypers and Austin Williams, *Manifesto: Towards a New Humanism in Architecture*, 2008, at <http://www.futurecities.org. uk/images/mantownhuman.pdf>.

4. Ford Madox Ford, in W. W. Hutchings, *London Town: Past and Present with a chapter on the Future in London by Ford Madox Hueffer, Volume II*, Cassell & Co., 1909, p. 1110.

5. Simon Sadler, *Archigram: Architecture Without Architecture*, MIT Press, 2005.

6. See Peter Hall, *Cities of Tomorrow*, Blackwell, 1996, and Neil Spiller, *Visionary Architecture: Blueprints of the Modern Imagination*, Thames & Hudson, 2007, for two comprehensive studies of visionary architecture and urbanism.

7. Urban Task Force, *Towards an Urban Renaissance*, UK Department of the Environment, Transport and the Regions, 1999.

8. Jeff Stein, 'Visionary American Architecture', in Nancy B. Solomon, ed., *Architecture: Celebrating the Past, Designing the Future*, Visual Reference Publications, 2008, p. 57.

9. Antonio Sant'Elia, *Manifesto of Futurist Architecture*, transl. from Italian, 1914, at <www.unknown.nu/futurism/architecture.html>.

10. David Ohana, *The Futurist Syndrome: Volume III of the Nihilist Order*, Sussex Academic Press, 2010, p. 54.

11. Christopher Wilk, ed., *Modernism: Designing a New World 1914–1939*, Victoria and Albert Museum, 2006.

12. Nathan Glazer, *From a Cause to a Style: Modernist Architecture's Encounter with the American City*, Princeton University Press, 2007.

13. Tim Jackson, *Prosperity without Growth: Economics for a Finite Planet*, Earthscan, 2009, p. 2.

14. Chandran Nair, *Consumptionomics: Asia's Role in Reshaping Capitalism and Saving the Planet*, Infinite Ideas, 2011, p. 16.

15. BBC News, 'Half of Humanity Set to Go Urban', 19 May 2005, at <news.bbc.co.uk/1/hi/sci/tech/4561183.stm>.

16. Hans Stimmann quoted in Alan Balfour, ed., 'World Cities BERLIN', Academy Editions, 1995.

17. Andreas Tzortzis, 'Berlin's Post-Wall Master Builder Retires', *New York Times*, 27 September 2006.

18. David Chipperfield, in Austin Williams, 'Talkback: David Chipperfield', NBS Learning Channels, 17 January 2011 at <www.youtube.com/user/FutureCities?feature=mhee#p/u/2/dehPdbW4aKQ>.

19. Sir Banister Fletcher quoted in Dan Cruikshank, ed., 'Sir Banister Fletcher's *A History of Architecture*', 20th edn, Architectural Press, 2001, p 1318.

20. Irene Murray, in Austin Williams, 'Adolf Loos', NBS Learning Channels, 1 March 2011, at <www.youtube.com/user/FutureCities?feature=mhee#p/u/8/9Kz6jWxOAq0>.

21. Rem Koolhaas, with Bruce Mau, 'What Ever Happened to Urbanism?', in *S,M,L,Xl, Oma*, Monicelli Press, 1995, pp. 959, 971.

22. Ibid., pp. 959, 971.

23. Ibid., pp. 959.

24. John Faherty, 'Arcosanti, Paolo Soleri Still Inspire', *Arizona Republic*, 22 August 2010.

25. Arcosanti, 'Arcosanti Project History', at <www.arcosanti.org/project/background/history/main.html>.

26. Jeffrey Cook quoted in Alastair Gordon, 'Deep in the Desert, No Longer Far Out', *New York Times*, 26 July 2001.

27. Alex Steffen, 'Recycling Arcosanti', *WorldChanging*, 3 June 2004, at <www.worldchanging.com/archives/000793.html>.

28. Dwayne Day, 'The God that failed', *Space Review, 18* May 2009, at <www.thespacereview.com/article/1376/1>.

29. Ibid.

30. Ibid.

31. Total capital investment in Dubai's manufacturing sector touched AED26.4 billion in 2005. Ameinfo, 8 November 2005, at <www.ameinfo.com/71335.html>.

32. Johann Hari, 'The Dark Side of Dubai', *Independent*, 7 April 2009.

33. 'Dubai Urban Area Structure Plan', GIS Department of Dubai Municipality, at <www.gis.gov.ae/portal/page/portal/GIS_PORTAL/E-STORE/FreE-Maps/Structure%20Plan.pdf>.

34. UAE Interact, '90 Per Cent of Dubai Will Be Urban by 2015', 4 February 2002, at <www.uaeinteract.com/docs/90_per_cent_of_Dubai_will_be_urban_by_2015/2960.htm>.

35. Lebbeus Woods, 'Delirious Dubai', 2008, at <lebbeuswoods. wordpress.com/2008/03/05/delirious-dubai>.
36. Mike Davis, 'Fear and Money in Dubai', *New Left Review* 41 (September–October 2006).
37. Mike Davis and Daniel Bertrand Monk, *Evil Paradises: Dreamworlds of Neoliberalism*, New Press, 2007.
38. Rem Koolhaas, *Delirious New York: A Retroactive Manifesto of Manhattan*, Monacelli Press, 1994.
39. Yasser Elsheshtawy, *Dubai: Behind an Urban Spectacle*, Routledge, 2009, p. 3.
40. Ibid.
41. Ibid.
42. Ibid
43. Final report of the Urban Task Force, *Towards an Urban Renaissance*, UK Department of the Environment, Transport and the Regions, 1999.
44. C. J. Lim and Ed Liu, *Smart-Cities and Eco-Warriors*, Routledge, 2010.

Conclusion
The Civilised City

Austin Williams

I am a citizen, neither of Athens or Greece, but of the world.

Socrates, in Plutarch's *Moralia*

As the contributions to this book have demonstrated, the city is not a straightforward entity. Manuel Castells says that 'defining urban meaning is a conflictive process'.[1] In 1937 the great urban theorist and historian Lewis Mumford posed the question, 'What is a City?', replying that 'in its complete sense [the city] is a geographical plexus, an economic organization, an institutional process, a theater of social action, and an aesthetic symbol of creative unity'.[2]

In 1905 the Modernist writer Ford Madox Ford posed the same question. After completing a number of forays into and around London – by bicycle, on foot, by bus – he asked himself, 'What is London?' and replied, with remarkable candour, that he still did not know. For all his exploration, he was none the wiser and could only describe it as the 'apotheosis of modern life'.[3] Ford, a man who would undoubtedly be labelled a 'psychogeographer' by today's Situationist guardians of urban emotional intelligence, or a 'flaneur' by those more poetically inclined (although Madox Ford was actually neither self-indulgent nor decadent enough, respectively, to merit the labels), was in fact simply an early urban sociologist. He roamed the streets, people-watching and trying to work out what different perspectives his observations could bring to the city. He could not define London because it was not a static entity. Writing at the end of the Victorian era and the beginning of the Georgian, he believed in the city's movement, its flux, its inherent lack of absolute certainty. He noted in a later essay that 'for a city to have a future it must grow', and that that future was 'very much in our hands'.[4]

His was an excited uncertainty, in which the future was unknown but he could not wait to see it. This was a mood of the time. Arriving in the city of Trieste in 1909 (the year of the *Futurist Manifesto*), Hermann Bahr, the Viennese playwright, said that he felt as if he were 'nowhere at all'.[5] This was a compliment: the city was an open book. As we saw in the debate on urban memory in Chapter 5, today's self-absorbed flaneurs are obsessed by their locality. The writer and broadcaster Laurie Taylor has observed that 'strolling aimlessly around towns and motorways has become an essential form of locomotion for today's urban intellectual'.[6] But unlike Madox Ford, contemporary exponents of psychogeography are desperate to preserve the 'essence' of their surroundings. Even though they acknowledge that 'people make places', it is the 'place' that takes primacy. In other words, at the centre of contemporary writings on the city is the environment; at the centre of earlier writings, I would suggest, was humanity. To his credit, the economist Edward Glaeser, writing in his excellent defence of urbanism in *The Triumph of the City*, recognises that 'we must free ourselves from our tendency to see cities as their buildings, and remember that the real city is made of flesh, not concrete'.[7]

Nevertheless, the suggestion that humans have a natural predisposition to congregate together in cities has a whiff of evolutionary psychology (EP) about it. Undoubtedly, utilising the ideas of his fellow Harvard professor Steven Pinker, Glaeser's appreciation of our 'urban species' goes too far towards conceiving of us naturally urban. In fact, what makes us human is our conscious actions as subjective agents of history; as Shakespeare once asked, 'What is the city but the people?'

An acquiescence to the mystical, EP-style agenda, which suggests that natural selection is generative of our identity, has become very popular – and very degraded. Jeremy Rifkin claims that 'our core nature is shown not to be rational, detached, acquisitive, aggressive and narcissistic, as Enlightenment philosophers claimed, but affectionate, highly social, co-operative and interdependent'. Robert M. Sapolsky, the author of 'Monkeyluv and Other Essays on Our Lives as Animals' asks, 'What are we to make of these correlations between environment and cultural beliefs and practices? Think of us humans as the primates that we are, and it makes perfect sense.'[8] However, think of us as humans able to transcend our environment, and it ceases to be a relevant analogy.

Richard Florida says that, in an increasingly globalised world, place is going to become more important. He believes that 'place exerts powerful influence over the jobs and careers we have access to, the people we meet and our "mating markets" and our ability to lead happy and fulfilled lives'.[9] Such urban fatalism may be written with the best possible intentions, but it can only reinforce a sense that humans play second fiddle to the places they inhabit. The proviso – or addendum – that these places are human constructs is small comfort.

Having failed to define a city, except to say that it is the embodiment of a metropolitan mindset and that it is a relationship of flux, this chapter will examine the notion of a civilised city. It then addresses the contemporary collapse of our ability to defend the city's civilising mission. Unfortunately, there is a mainstream opinion that views civilisation as a Western concept, rather than a universal construct that benefits humanity as a whole, as opposed to only the West. There is thus a tendency on the part of some to invent a non-western, particularist view of progress, which, at its limits, celebrates difference through the prism of anti-westernism. Or, as Hamm and Smandych say, with an ironic nod to Eurocentric, post-modern linguistic acrobatics: 'There are emerging points of resistance to the hegemony and growth points of new culture outside the Eurocentric realm.'[10]

This chapter seeks to explore the idea that cities are engines of social as well as intellectual creativity – that they are created by humanity, for humanity. In Mumford's classic *The City in History*, he describes the city as a place of civilisation. In his interpretation, the nomadic, hunter-gatherer tribes of prehistory had struggled merely to survive in their harsh, peripatetic world. 'City' settlements caused humans to emerge from their barbarous relationship with nature and develop an ordered, cultured, social stability. Conversely, in his more modern, misanthropic and polemical account, Alan Weisman insists that humans 'vainly or disingenuously pretend [that] our codes of civilization transcend'[11] the barbarity of nature.

This chapter sets itself the task of defending the civilised city. So, first of all, what do we mean by civilisation?

WHAT IS CIVILISATION?

If the city is hard to define, then the concept of civilisation seems even more slippery. At the beginning of his BBC series, *Civilisation*, aired in the 1960s, Kenneth Clark asked himself the question: 'What is civilisation?' to which he replied: 'I don't know. I can't define it in abstract terms; but I think I can recognise it when I see it'.[12] His starting point was that 'creative power and the enlargement of the human faculties'[13] were the hallmark of civilised progress. Civilisation was not a natural state, and his observations on the human condition at the time gave him no cause to assume complacently that civilisation would necessarily survive. If it was not nurtured, he said, civilisation might founder.

John Armstrong, in his book *In Search of Civilization: Remaking a Tarnished Idea*, also suggests that the object of his enquiry is easier to recognise than to define, partly because of its dialectical nature. Civilisation is not purely material (for example, in improvements to physical health, or economic growth), but neither is it solely about high art. Rather, it is about the concurrence of both. On one hand, there is the higher cultural, order – a value-driven, social commitment – which profoundly shapes the way we view civilisation; but there is also the dimension of quantifiable economic growth, and what he calls 'heroic materialism'. It is apparent not only that words like 'civilisation', 'development', 'progress', and so on, are hard to pin down; they have in fact been challenged and criticised since the dawn of the Enlightenment. But it is only in the relatively recent period that their conventional interpretation has lacked a robust defence.

So the defence of civilisation is predicated not only on the fact that it is better than barbarism, but also on the claim that it is the essence of a 'life well lived'. As Karl Marx explained in the *Grundrisse*: 'Hunger is hunger, but the hunger gratified by cooked meat eaten with a knife and fork is a different hunger from that which bolts down raw meat with the aid of hand, nail and tooth.' There, within one sentence, we see the positive direction – but incomplete project – of civilisational progress.

The idea of 'civilisation' incorporates the gains of history that have coloured the preceding chapters of this book. It includes the improvements in the quality and standards of life – the benefits of social engagement, of mixed populations and public interaction, of a free society with equality of ambition, of critical thinking, of freedom of expression and enquiry, of rights to assembly and individual autonomy, of conscious human engagement and progressive thinking, of collective action within civil society, of increased wealth and new opportunities, of improved and extended mobility, of risk-taking and limit-challenging, of reason over superstition, of human aspiration over natural barriers, of the cosmopolitan and metropolitan mindset over parochial values. These elements together identify a conception of civilisation given expression in the city.

The importance of the debate today resides in its defence of the core progressive values of civilisation that are under attack from a dialectical coalition of relativism and intellectual timidity.

Definitional certainty is overrated, as the mantra of sustainability will attest. As one early defender of the 'S' label admitted: 'Despite being clearly and meticulously defined, in terms both scientific and social, [sustainability] was regularly accused of promoting vagueness, hiding a green political agenda, hiding a pro-business agenda or attempting to be "all things to all people".'[14] That said, the notion of sustainability has still evolved into the dominant political and economic frame of reference in current use, and provides an agreed starting point for architects and urbanists. Civilisation ought to be seen in the same light – as an all-embracing state of moral reason. However, the lack of definitional niceties should not be confused with an inability to provide a clear perception of what it stands for. Failure to come to a universal consensus on the meaning of a term should not be used as an excuse for abandoning it as a principle of action. Clarity is still fundamentally important, and we should not wilfully play with obfuscations as way of avoiding difficult arguments. This was the mistake of Nathaniel Wei, the man charged with delivering the Big Society, who revelled in the fact that 'for many of us the idea of Big Society can be confusing. This is not necessarily a bad thing.'[15] Wrong. Confusion – and more importantly, the cynical use that is made of it – is a bad thing: it is disingenuous, evasive and cowardly. By the end of his epic televisual essay, Kenneth Clark concluded that 'it is lack of confidence, more than anything else, that kills a civilisation'.[16]

Unfortunately, the creeping inability to argue a confident defence of civilisation and the civilised city has also left itself open to the opportunism of the relativist to suggest that it is all a matter of opinion. This sense of moral equivalence between civilisation and illiberalism (wherein the population is illiberally 'nudged' towards behaving in a correct and civilised manner) is a dangerous turn. We saw in Chapter 6, for example, that the rise of restrictions on liberty does not always have to show itself in authoritarian ways; so it is important to assert – and reassert – that civilisation is better than the alternatives. For Ayaan Hirsi Ali, for example, 'That Western civilization is superior is not simply [an] opinion but a reality'.[17] A bald statement such as this has the merit of clarity, hopefully making it easier to engage critically with the concepts.

DEFENSIVE ARGUMENTS

Speaking about the development of Musheireb, a new town in Doha, its architects are keen to stress that the project is not imposing a western-style agenda on the Qatari skyline, admitting that they want to avoid a 'banal, homogenising globalism'.[18]

There are other contemporary examples of this kind of defensiveness – or even contrition – about the impact of western mores on less developed societies, recently articulated mostly by western commentators. The design of Musheireb, for instance, is said to be progressing at a sedate pace, and proudly 'looks to traditional wisdoms'.[19] All too often, a perception exists today that the developing world has much to teach us, particularly on the question of our relationship to nature, our pace of life, and a general humility towards material development. Take the 'city in a village' concept, which creates 'not an urban center but a sustainable village with town-like diversity that provides an array of jobs and employs low-cost, environmentally sound technologies and watershed management approaches to sustain what is essentially village life'.[20]

In a period of shifting geopolitical power, emerging economies are staking a claim for their place in the civilised sun. Islamic groups point out the debt owed to them for civilisational advances in science, mathematics, astronomy and medicine. All true, although the intervening 1,000 years have not lived up to that early promise. China's stated aim of 'non-interference' has meant that it has held back from making excessive cultural claims (although Guangzhou, its third-wealthiest metropolis, won the national 'Civilised City' award by enforcing rules against spitting and talking loudly). One Chinese report states that '[w]omen wearing red armbands patrol the streets and pick up cigarette butts. Volunteer crossing guards with yellow flags and whistles make sure people wait for green lights. Beggars, even those with legs withered by polio, are banished from their usual haunts.'[21] This is not the model that we have tried to champion throughout this book, but, given that the 2010 Shanghai Expo's slogan was 'Better City, Better Life' – coupled with its branding as a 'City of Harmony' – it is clear that China recognises that economic development is not enough, and that there is a role for systematically improving people's living standards and quality of life.

A number of Indian commentators are keen to stress their difference, in an assertion of the break with their colonial past. Famously, when Mahatma Gandhi was asked what he thought of western civilisation, he replied that he thought 'it would be a good idea'. Less playfully, he also claimed that 'the tendency of Indian civilization is to elevate the moral being, that of the western civilization is to propagate immorality'.[22] In Gandhi's footsteps, Professor Anil Gupta, in Ahmedabad, insists on intellectual egalitarianism, countering western big business with the previously untapped potential of villages. But Professor

Ashish Nandy, at the Centre for the Study of Developing
Societies, in Delhi, is a more forthright critic of modernity, and
seeks to promote the 'non-modern' cultures of the Third World.
This sectarian rejection of all the global gains of history compels
them both to invent an alternative ('other ways of constructing
the past'), which for Nandy is predicated on 'multivalent and
amorphous' myths, which allow 'chaos and plurality of spiritual
belief [to be] the binding cement of this civilisation'.[23]

The universalising gains of progress – much developed and
nurtured in the West – have become particularised by such
postures, which refuse to countenance the idea that the benefits
of civilisation listed earlier in this chapter are not the province
of just one country or region. Civilisational gains arising from
philosophical and physical battles in the West benefit everyone.
Socratic thought is not an out-dated, slave-owners' fancy, but
is perennially relevant, and has influenced thinkers ever since.

Such is the world of ideas, and the civilised urban arenas in
which they find expression. There is little that an isolated village
individual can do to benefit the world, without his or her having
entered the arena developed by the collective wisdom of urban
humanity. Standing on the shoulders of giants – giants of the
western canon – is imperative. And that's just how it is.

THE CIVILISING UNDERCURRENT

Liberalism rests on the ideal that individuals should be free to pursue
a diversity of ends of life. I explain and adopt liberal individualism as a
key normative pillar supporting an ideal global Collective Management
framework in which citizens are free to pursue their own ends as long as
they do not infringe on the rights of others to do the same.[24]

So wrote Saif Gaddafi in his London School of Economics PhD
thesis in 2007, blissfully unaware of the storm gathering under
the cover of citizens' rights. As I write, in early 2011, the revolts
and rebellions happening in the Middle East and North Africa
are emblematic of the human hunger for the universal prinicples
of progress and democracy, so long denied to them. Such turmoil

also reflects the city's potential to give people – what might be called the 'urban proletariat' – power and a voice. Protest in the metropolitan heartland is the physical realisation of the phrase 'speaking truth to power'; after all, the city is where power resides, whether that of the ruling elites or of the revolting, downtrodden masses.

'Urban proletariat' is clearly imprecise. These have not been struggles of the working classes against the bourgeouisie, but are clearly the struggle of the persecuted and the unfree against their tormentors. Gaddafi's dictum, for example, that 'execution is the fate of anyone who forms a political party',[25] is a sharp reminder of the reasons why national quietude has prevailed in Libya for over 40 years, but also of source of the eruption of anger in 2011. It is a striking example of the obstacles facing the desire for change in a one-party state: the discomfort, or even death, resulting for some of those who participate – and those who do not – act as timely reminders of current prospects for the onward march for progress. Such was the argument advanced in the preceding chapters – all of which dealt with urban progress, and hinted that pain and suffering are unfortunate, ugly but necessary parts of the movement of history.

In several countries of the Middle East and North Africa, it has been only by mass collective action that change has been possible – reliant as it is on large concentrations of people. For all the hype about a virtual 'Facebook revolution', these protests relied on the physical imperative: the massed ranks of real people dedicated – by strength of collective purpose as well as by physical force – to effecting change. Geographer Mario Polese asserts that 'human contact is more important than ever in the age of information technology, and people will continue to seek places where they can share ideas, make transactions, and pursue their dreams. There's nowhere better to do these things than big cities.'[26] It is thus hardly surprising that the so-called Arab Spring uprisings began in Tunisia, which is the most urbanised country on the African continent (52 per cent of its population live in cities).

Clearly, this is not an inevitable process. The simple fact that the population is urban does not mean that it will necessarily protest; in fact, a number of highly urbanised countries of northern Africa may yet remain stable, precisely because of the complex mix of politics, religion and wealth at play. Indeed, we have seen, there is nothing deterministic about 'place' – nothing about any given region automatically engenders radicalism. But there are material factors within those regions that are significant influences. Dr Omar Elbendak of the University of Alfateh in Tripoli notes that the Maghreb region

> is the most urbanised sub-region in Africa and urban growth in Arab Maghreb society is partially the result of rural–urban migration, but natural urban growth and reclassification account for more than 70 per cent of urban development … This migration trend can be attributed to the greater opportunities, in terms of education and employment that are to be found in cities.[27]

Modern urbanisation in the northern states of Africa has occurred because of the development of capitalist social relations. Much of the move from village to city is a function of industrialisation and the growth of the economy (although there is a dialectical relationship at play: the influx of people is the very factor that has allowed the economy in some of these regions to expand so rapidly). Urban growth has also been accelerated by the inward migration of people escaping the conflicts in neighbouring countries to commercially more dynamic sectors. Nevertheless, urbanisation has fundamentally gone hand in hand with the modernisation of various pockets of the region.

The country with the highest rate of urbanisation between 1950 and 2000 was Libya. Its urban population is now six times higher than when Gaddafi came to power in 1969, and – remarkably – fifteen times what it was in 1960, reflecting the greatest urban transformation of any Arab Maghreb country. Dr Elbendak records that 'in lower Libya the 1950 urban population was about 193 times bigger than that of 45 years earlier – a rural increase of 3,000,882'.[28]

Egypt's urban population is growing by 1.6 million per year, reflecting a growth rate of 4 per cent per annum. Its urban population has increased six times in the last 60 years. The head of architecture at Alexandria University says that such 'rapid urbanization coinciding with the longest period of economic prosperity in modern Egypt has created a huge demand for urban housing and [a] spreading of urban informality, by which more than 80 per cent of housing constructed in the last three decades in Egypt [was] illegal'.[29] The fact that the housing minister at the time, Ahmed al-Maghraby, was said to have had a personal fortune of more than US$6 billion cannot have helped soothe the protesters' anger.[30] The effective overthrow of the regime (though unaccompanied as yet by any revolutionary social transformation) is an impressive feat given that Egypt has the tenth-largest military in the world, with more than 460,000 troops and an annual defence budget of $2.5 billion.

Writing of the architectural history of twentieth-century western dictatorships, the director of the Design Museum, Deyan Sudjic, says that huge urban squares were 'the physical embodiment and a metaphorical representation of a new political order'.[31] So it is in the Arab world, where totalitarian and authoritarian heads of state – from Libya's Gaddafi to Tunisia's Ben Ali to Egypt's Mubarak – have harboured monumental civic pretensions. But their central plazas – from Tahrir Square in Cairo to Kasbah Square in Tunis; from Red Square to Tianenman Square; from Wenceslas Square to Kim Il-sung Square – were all sham examples of public space. They were public spaces without a public; many were civic parade grounds in the absence of a civil society.

The officially sanctioned 'public' mobilisations that were regularly staged in these arenas were truly exposed as such when these squares were commandeered by the *real* public – both in 1989, and more recently during the Arab Spring of 2011. Suddenly, genuine public space was brought into being. Once again, these locations became arenas of public autonomy – places where individuals come together without the official sanction of the state. They were robust arenas of political discourse.

As political commentator Josie Appleton notes, public space is 'a space that [is] neither the market nor the state – where people collaborate informally and freely with one another'. It requires the city (*polis*) to be the collective embodiment of the people (*demos*).

A CITIZEN'S AGORA

The central place of humanity in the city is a defining feature of civilisation. Peter Hall notes that 'the biggest and most cosmopolitan cities ... have throughout history been the places that ignited the sacred flame of the human intelligence and the human imagination'.[32] Author and academic Joel Kotkin has claimed that cities 'represent the ultimate handiwork of our imagination as a species'.[33] Commenting on Lewis Mumford's musings on the city, the editor of the *Architectural Record* pointed out that Mumford 'saw the urban experience as an integral component in the development of human culture and the human personality'. Against such transcendent claims, Lord Rogers's edict that 'people make cities and cities make citizens'[34] pales by comparison.

His was the New Labour variant of the current coalition government's Big Society of 'big citizens', according to which cities are viewed merely as social policy devices for the achievement of desired outcomes. Such instrumentalism – in which urban places are invested in in order to create civilised citizens, responsible citizens, or correct citizens – is one of the canonical legitimising devices of architects and urban designers today. It is usual to hear cities described in much more anodyne, technical terms, in which the word 'city' is rarely spoken without an accompanying proviso or prefix, such as 'low-carbon', 'smart', 'compact', 'inclusive', 'safe', 'healthy', or 'sustainable'. All of these hedges tend to justify and excuse, rather than explain, the public essence of a city, and all aim to engineer the citizen into existence. 'The urban utopia', says one conference on urban design, 'must be capable of supporting high-density living, yet foster community well-being and also be sustainable and ecologically sound.'[35] The autonomous individual – the Kantian 'free agent' – is noticeably absent.

The real virtuous citizen is a familiar figure in political philosophy. As an active subject, he or she retains few recognisable connections to the passive objects of today. In Plato's *Apology*, Socrates places the city of Athens on trial in order to ascertain the nature of civic rule and political authority. His Academy was established to develop citizens for positions of public office, through the gateway of educational excellence. Today, by contrast, education is a sycophantic contrivance designed to achieve a defined, prescribed citizen, rather than aspiring to create philosopher-kings. This book dares to suggest that we need to learn how to challenge orthodoxies and take some risks. After all, a civilised city of free citizens can only exist in a framework of genuine critical engagement.

NOTES

1. Manuel Castells in Alexander R. Cuthbert, eds, *Designing Cities: Critical Readings in Urban Design*, Blackwell, 2003, p. 25.
2. Lewis Mumford, 'What is a City?', *Architectural Record* LXXXII (November 1937), p. 94.
3. Ford Madox Ford, *The Soul of London: A Survey of a Modern City*, Everyman, 1995, p. 111.
4. Ford Madox Ford, in W. W. Hutchings, *London Town: Past and Present with a Chapter on the Future in London by Ford Madox Hueffer, Volume II*, Cassell & Co., 1909, p. 1110.
5. Jan Morris, *Trieste and the Meaning of Nowhere*, Da Capo Press, 2002, p. 17.
6. Laurie Taylor, 'Endgame: Walk On By', *New Humanist* 123: 5 (September–October 2008).
7. Edward Glaeser, *The Triumph of the City: How Our Greatest Invention Makes Us Richer, Smarter, Greener, Healthier And Happier*, Macmillan, 2011, p. 15.
8. Robert M. Sapolsky, 'What Makes Us Who We Are?' *Independent*, 19 October 2005.
9. Richard Florida, *Who's Your City? How the Creative Economy is Making the Place Where You Live the Most Important Decision of Your Life*, Basic Books, 2008.

10. Bernd Hamm and Russell Smandych, eds, *Cultural Imperialism: Essays on the Practical Economy of Cultural Domination*, Broadview Press, 2005, p. 49.
11. Alan Weisman, *The World Without Us*, Virgin Books, 2008, p. 98.
12. Kenneth Clark, *Civilisation*, Penguin, 1987, p. 17.
13. Ibid., p. 227.
14. Alan AtKisson, *Believing Cassandra: How to Be an Optimist in a Pessimist's World*, Chelsea Green Publishing, 1999, p. 134.
15. Nathaniel Wei, 'Why Big Society Can Be Confusing – And Why This is Alright', Big Society blog, 18 June 2010, at <www.thebigsociety. net/?p=242&utm_source=twitterfeed&utm_medium=twitter>.
16. Clark, *Civilisation*, p. 246.
17. Ayaan Hirsi Ali, *Nomad: From Islam to America: A Personal Journey Through the Clash of Civilizations*, Simon & Schuster, 2010, p. 245.
18. Felix Mara, 'Doha', *Architects' Journal*, 17 February 2011, p. 24.
19. Ibid., p. 26.
20. Geeta Pradhan and Rajesh K. Pradhan, 'Hybrid Cities: A Basis for Hope', *The Bridge: Earth Systems Engineering* 31: 1 (Spring 2001), p. 22.
21. William Foreman, 'Chinese Metropolis Seeks to Clean Up Its Image', *LA Times*, 13 September 2009.
22. Robert H. Taylor, *The Idea of Freedom in Asia and Africa: The Making of Modern Freedom*, Stanford University Press, 2002, p. 132.
23. Staff reporter, 'Concerted Effort to Historicise Indian Epic Culture: Ashis Nandy', *Hindu Times*, 19 February 2011.
24. Saif al-Islam al-Gaddafi, 'The Role of Civil Society in the Democratisation of Global Governance Institutions: From "Soft Power" to Collective Decision-Making?', Phd, London School of Economics and Political Science, September 2007, p. 71.
25. Mohamed Eljahmi, 'Libya and the US: Qadhafi Unrepentant', *Middle East Quarterly* XIII: 1 (Winter 2006), pp. 11–20.
26. Mario Polese, 'Why Big Cities Matter More than Ever', *City Journal* 20: 4 (Autumn 2010).
27. Dr Omar Elbendak, 'Urbanisation in Arab Maghreb Region: An Overview', *Journal of Human Sciences* 7: 44 (January 2010), p. 5.
28. Ibid., p. 8.

29. Ahmed M. Soliman, 'Remodel Urban Development In Egypt: A Future Vision', US–Egypt Workshop on Space Technology and Geo-Information for Sustainable Development, Cairo, 14–17 June 2010, p. 3.

30. Amina Abdul Salam, 'What Happened under Egypt's Nazif', *Gazette Online*, 20 February 2011, at <213.158.162.45/~egyptian/index.php?action=news&id=15265&title=What%20happened%20under%20Egypt's%20Nazif>.

31. Deyan Sudjic, *The Edifice Complex: The Architecture of Power*, Penguin, 2011.

32. Peter Hall, *Cities in Civilization*, Phoenix Giant, 1998, p. 11.

33. Joel Kotkin, *The City: A Global History*, Weidenfield & Nicholson, 2005, p. xviii.

34. Roy Porter, *London: A Social History*, Harvard University Press, 1998, p. 7.

35. *Economist* conference, 'Creating Tomorrow's Liveable Cities: Urban Planning in a Cold Climate', 19 January 2011, at <www.economistconferences.co.uk/event/creating-tomorrows-liveable-cities/3832>.

Further Reading

Introduction: The Paradoxical City

Marshal Berman, *All That Is Solid Melts Into Air*, Verso, 1983.

Edward Glaeser, *Triumph of the City: How Our Greatest Invention Makes Us Richer, Smarter, Greener, Healthier and Happier*, Macmillan, 2011.

Joel Kotkin, *The Next Hundred Million: America in 2050*, Penguin, 2010.

Ford Madox Ford, *The Soul of London: A Survey of a Modern City*, Everyman, 1995 [1905].

Thomas Sieverts, *Cities Without Cities: Between Place and World, Space and Time, Town and Country*, Routledge, 2003.

1.   The Dynamic City

Peter Hessler, *Oracle Bones: A Journey Between China and the West*, John Murray, 2006.

Doug Saunders, *Arrival City: How the Largest Migration in History is Reshaping Our World*, William Heinemann, 2010.

Robin Visser, *Cities Surround the Countryside, Urban Aesthetics in Postsocialist China*, Duke University Press, 2010.

Wang Hui, *China's New Order: Society, Politics, and Economy in Transition*, ed. Theodore Huters, Harvard University Press, 2006.

Li Zhang, *In Search of Paradise, Middle-Class Living in a Chinese Metropolis*, Cornell University Press, 2010.

2.   The Emerging City

Leslie T. Chang, *Factory Girls: Voices from the Heart of Modern China*, Picador, 2008.

Mike Davies, *Planet of Slums*, Verso, 2006.

Bregtje van der Haak, dir., *Lagos Wide and Close: An Interactive Journey in to and Exploding City*, Submarine, in co-production with VPRO, 2005 (DVD).

Gyan Prakash, *Mumbai Fables*, Princeton University Press, 2010.

Edward K. Spann, *The New Metropolis: New York City, 1840–1857*, Columbia University Press, 1981.

3. The Crowded City

Alessandro Magnoli Bocchi, *World Development Report 2009: Reshaping Economic Geography*, World Bank, 2009.

Frank Furedi, *Population and Development: A Critical Introduction*, Polity, 1997.

Thomas Malthus, *An Essay on the Principle of Population, as it Affects the Future Improvement of Society, with Remarks on the Speculations of Mr Godwin, M. Condorcet, and Other Writers*, J. Johnson, 1798.

Fred Pearce, *Peoplequake: Mass Migration, Aging Nations and the Coming Population Crash*, Eden Project Books, 2010.

Matt Ridley, *The Rational Optimist: How Prosperity Evolves*, Fourth Estate, 2010.

4. The Planned City

Hilary Ballon and Kenneth T. Jackson, eds, *Robert Moses and the Modern City: The Transformation of New York*, W.W. Norton & Co., 2007.

Robert Goodman, *After the Planners*, Routledge, 1972.

Ebenezer Howard, *Garden Cities of To-Morrow*, reprinted and ed. with a Preface by F. J. Osborn, Faber & Faber, 1946 [1902].

Erik Larson, *The Devil in the White City: Murder, Magic, and Madness at the Fair that Changed America*, Vintage, 2004.

Colin Ward, *Cotters and Squatters: The Hidden History of Housing*, Five Leaves Publications, 2002.

5. The Historic City

Walter Benjamin, *The Arcades Project*, Harvard University Press, 2002.

M. Christine Boyer, *The City of Collective Memory: Its Historical Imagery and Architectural Entertainments*, MIT Press, 1996.

David Runciman, *Political Hypocrisy: The Mask of Power, from Hobbes to Orwell and Beyond*, Princeton University Press, 2008.

Edmund White, *The Flaneur: A Stroll Through the Paradoxes of Paris*, Bloomsbury, 2008.

Gary Younge, *Who are We – And Should it Matter in the 21st Century?*, Viking, 2010.

6.   The Sanitised City

Hannah Arendt, *On Revolution*, Viking, 1963.

Anna Minton, *Ground Control: Fear and Happiness in the Twenty-First Century*, Penguin, 2009.

Brian Monteith, *The Bully State: The End of Tolerance*, Free Society, 2009.

William H. Whyte, *The Social Life of Small Urban Spaces*, Municipal Art Society of New York, 1979 (see <vimeo.com/5298850>.)

Richard J. Williams, *The Anxious City: British Urbanism in the Late 20th Century*, Routledge, 2004.

7.   The Eco-City

Stewart Brand, *Whole Earth Discipline: An Ecopragmatist Manifesto*, Atlantic, 2010.

C. J. Lim and Ed Liu, *Smart-Cities and Eco-Warriors*, Routledge, 2010.

Friedrich Engels, *The Condition of the Working Class in England*, Penguin Classics, 2006.

Shannon May, 'Ecological Citizenship and a Plan for Sustainable Development', *City* 12: 2 (Summer 2008), pp. 237–44.

Suketu Mehta, *Maximum City: Bombay Lost and Found*, Headline Review, 2005.

8.   The Visionary City

Marie-Ange Brayes, Jane Alison, Frederic Migayrou and Neil Spiller, *Future City: Experiment and Utopia in Architecture*, Thames & Hudson, 2007.

Alex Danchev, *100 Artists' Manifestos: From the Futurists to the Stuckists*, Penguin Classics, 2011.

Peter Hall, *Cities of Tomorrow*, Blackwell Publishers, 1996.

Simon Sadler, *Archigram: Architecture Without Architecture*, MIT Press, 2005.

Manfredo Tafuri, *Architecture and Utopia: Design and Capitalist Development*, MIT Press, 1976.

9. The Civilised City

David Armstrong, *In Search of Civilization: Remaking a Tarnished Idea*, Allen Lane, 2009.

Kenneth Clark, *Civilisation: A Personal View*, BBC/John Murray, 1971.

Dolan Cummings, ed., *Debating Humanism*, Imprint Academic, 2006.

Paul Mason, *Live Working or Die Fighting: How the Working Class Went Global*, Harvill Secker, 2007.

Richard Reeves, *John Stuart Mill: Victorian Firebrand*, Atlantic Books, 2008.

Contributors

Alastair Donald is associate director of the Future Cities Project. He has worked in urban policy and urban design, and is now researching mobility and space at the Martin Centre for Architectural and Urban Studies, University of Cambridge. He was convenor of the national conference *Minimum... or Maximum Cities?* and mantownhuman's *Challenging the Orthodoxies* debates. He co-edited *The Future of Community* (Pluto 2008).

Patrick Hayes works for the Institute of Ideas and current affairs magazine *spiked*, having previously been the head of research and development for the publishers of the *Times Educational Supplement* and *Times Higher Education*. He has explored over 50 countries across six continents, and produced a series of films on location in India and Nepal. He has an Executive MBA from Henley Business School, and has written a chapter for *A Lecturer's Guide to Further Education* (Oxford University Press).

Alan Hudson is director of Oxford University's Leadership Programmes for China. The programmes include the Advanced Leadership Development Programme, for those national ministers charged with the strategic implementation of the 11th Five Year Plan for a *xiaokang*, or 'well balanced society' of economic development and social justice. He has wide experience in both quantitative and qualitative research and analysis, and has acted as consultant in the public, private and voluntary sectors.

Steve Nash studied seventeenth-century political radicalism at the time of the English Civil War, then moved to the US to coordinate a grassroots citizen group founded by Ralph Nader. Moving back to London, he worked in urban regeneration with various charities and local government agencies. He is currently overseeing improvements to public sector processes.

Michael Owens is an associate director of DPP SHAPE, a creative urban regeneration and planning company. He is also a doctoral student at the University of Salford School for the Built and Human Environment. He has over 30 years of experience in urban strategy, policy and delivery, specialising in the socio-economic and political dimensions of urban change.

Tony Pierce has 20 years' experience as director/head of service in planning, property, engineering, surveying, housing and policy departments. At the time of writing, he advises the Mayor of London and Croydon Council on how best to build a new, 20,000-strong community in Croydon town centre. He is the co-founder of the Croydon Salon.

Karl Sharro is an architect and writer based in London, where he is a team leader designing a city in Qatar. Karl has practised architecture in London and Beirut, and taught for five years at the Department of Architecture at the American University of Beirut.

Austin Williams is the director of the Future Cities Project and lecturer in architecture at Xi'an Jiaotong–Liverpool University, Suzhou, China. He was previously the technical editor at the *Architects' Journal* and transport correspondent with the *Daily Telegraph*. He convenes the Bookshop Barnies, and was the founder of mantownhuman and the Critical Subjects architecture and design winter school. He is an independent filmmaker, writer and illustrator, and author of *Enemies of Progress*.

Index